Hannah Riddell

Hannah Riddell

AN ENGLISHWOMAN IN JAPAN

Julia Boyd

With a Foreword by
HRH The Princess of Wales

CHARLES E. TUTTLE COMPANY
Rutland, Vermont & Tokyo, Japan

To John and our children
who with (mostly) good humour shared
hearth and home with Hannah for two years

(*Frontispiece*). Hannah with one of her beloved dogs.

Published by the Charles E. Tuttle Company, Inc.
of Rutland, Vermont & Tokyo, Japan
with editorial offices at
2-6 Suido 1-chome, Bunkyo-ku, Tokyo 112

LCC Card No. 95-61324
ISBN 0-8048-2049-x

First edition, 1996

Printed in Japan

Contents

List of Illustrations   7

Foreword by HRH The Princess of Wales   9

CHAPTER 1. Setting Out   11

CHAPTER 2. Beginnings   14

CHAPTER 3. Bankrupt   19

CHAPTER 4. Liverpool   23

CHAPTER 5. An Exotic New World   27

CHAPTER 6. Christian Pioneers   33

CHAPTER 7. The Language   38

CHAPTER 8. Posting   44

CHAPTER 9. Kumamoto   50

CHAPTER 10. Leprosy   56

CHAPTER 11. Hannah   64

CHAPTER 12. Visitors   68

CHAPTER 13. Launching the Hospital   71

CHAPTER 14. Completion   79

CHAPTER 15. Ada   99

CONTENTS

CHAPTER 16. *Conflict*   107

CHAPTER 17. *Battle Lines*   112

CHAPTER 18. *Defeat*   120

CHAPTER 19. *Going Solo*   125

CHAPTER 20. *The Policeman's Friend*   131

CHAPTER 21. *The Big Time*   136

CHAPTER 22. *Theories*   142

CHAPTER 23. *Daily Life*   149

CHAPTER 24. *Karuizawa*   154

CHAPTER 25. *New Horizons*   158

CHAPTER 26. *Waters of Hell*   173

CHAPTER 27. *Okinawa*   179

CHAPTER 28. *Old Age*   183

CHAPTER 29. *Hard Times*   189

CHAPTER 30. *Pain and Healing*   194

Postscript   201

Notes   207

Bibliography   211

Acknowledgements   213

MAP
on pages 42–43

{6}

List of Illustrations

(*Frontispiece*). Hannah with one of her dogs.

 1. Mrs. Riddle, Hannah's mother.   81
 2. Hannah's study in Russell House.   81
 3. Women refuelling a ship.   82
 4. A turn-of-the-century postcard image of Japan.   82
 5. Missionaries, including Grace Nott, Hannah, and the Reverend Albert Fuller.   82
 6. Mount Aso.   83
 7. A Gifu village destroyed by the 1891 earthquake.   83
 8. Grace Nott in November 1890.   84
 9. Hannah in early 1891.   84
10. A view of Kumamoto from the summit of Hanaokayama.   84–85
11. The Fifth Higher School.   85
12. A victim of leprosy.   86
13. Stone steps at the Honmyoji temple.   86
14. The Japan Church Missionary Society Conference of 1894.   87
15. Ada Hannah Wright in 1897.   87
16. John Brandram.   87
17. Mary Brandram.   87
18. Katherine Tristram.   87
19. Bishop Henry Evington.   87
20. Albert Fuller.   87
21. Ada with two "Bible women."   88
22. A Japanese policeman accosted by British tourists.   88

23. Missionaries selling Testaments. 88
24. Hannah with fellow lady missionaries at Karuizawa. 89
25. The main street of Karuizawa in the 1900s. 89
26, 27. Dr. Shunsuke Miyake and the nurse Tamako Mitsui. 90
28. The opening ceremony of the Kaishun Hospital. 90
29. Two young patients at the Kaishun Hospital. 91
30. The hospital laboratory surrounded by cherry trees. 91
31. Count Shigenobu Okuma. 92
32. Viscount Eiichi Shibusawa. 92
33. The Bankers' Club, Tokyo. 92
34. Sir Claude MacDonald. 93
35. Hannah wearing the Medal of the Blue Ribbon. 93
36. The Imperial Hotel, Tokyo. 93
37. Hannah's dogs waiting in a jinrikisha. 94
38. Hannah's house at 436 Furushinyashiki. 94
39. Malcolm, an American patient at the hospital. 95
40. The Kaishun Hospital baseball team. 95
41. A patient walking along the hospital avenue. 96
42. Hannah in old age with tennis-playing patients. 96
43. Empress Dowager Teimei. 161
44. Female patients taking exercise. 162
45. The laboratory at the Kaishun Hospital. 162
46. Eight patients who were baptised by the Bishop of London. 163
47. Hannah with the Bishop of London and his party. 163
48. Hannah shortly before her death. 164
49. Hannah's funeral. 164
50. Ada and the hospital staff in the early 1930s. 165
51. Ada with a Special Messenger from Empress Dowager Teimei
   and his entourage. 165
52. A dedication from Helen Keller. 166
53. The closure of the Kaishun Hospital. 166
54. Ada with the children of leprosy patients. 167
55. Ada shortly before her death. 167
56. The author talking to former patients of the hospital. 168
57. The ceremony to mark the inauguration of the Riddell-Wright
   Memorial Society. 168

KENSINGTON PALACE

Travelling as Patron of The Leprosy Mission to many parts of the world, I have seen for myself the cruel way in which lives can be affected by leprosy. But, like so many others, I have also found among lepers and those who care for them some of the most courageous and inspiring people anyone could have been privileged to meet. It is of such a person and those she sought to help that Julia Boyd has written in this moving account of Hannah Riddell's life and work. The setting is Japan, but such a story of endurance and compassion has many parallels throughout history. Sadly, and perhaps surprisingly, it is a story whose message is still relevant wherever people live in the shadow of leprosy in our world today.

Diana

August, 1995

CHAPTER 1

Setting Out

On 14 November 1890 the SS *Denbighshire* sailed out of Southampton bound for Japan. On board five young women were leaving behind the security of middle-class Victorian England for a country on the other side of the world about which they knew almost nothing but where they had every intention of spending the rest of their lives. If the ladies faced an uncertain future, they nevertheless carried in their hearts and minds the unshakeable conviction that their Christian values—those of the Church of England—were the right ones, and that it was their personal mission to bring this Truth to the Japanese people.

At thirty-five Hannah Riddell was the oldest of the group—and the tallest. With her great height and strong, handsome features she was a commanding presence, radiating confidence and energy. But it was not just her physical appearance that marked her out as different from the others. Unlike the majority of young women missionaries recruited in the late nineteenth century, Hannah had earned her own living and support-ed a family. The responsibilities she had shouldered since her early twenties and the problems with which she had been forced to grapple gave her a self-reliance not normally expected of genteel ladies in Eng-land at that time but which was to prove vital in the coming years.

The five ladies, all recently enlisted, were going to Japan under the auspices of The Church Missionary Society (CMS), which had only two years before decided the time was ripe to send single women into the foreign field. Hannah had badly wanted to go to India, where for many years her father had served with the British army, but the CMS, keen to respond to the Japanese mission's urgent request for female workers, posted her instead to Japan.

What image of Japan did the new recruits carry with them as they set out on their great enterprise? They knew that Japan was exotic and quaint, a country filled with cherry blossom, which was safe, and geishas, which were not. They may have seen pictures in magazines of elegant women clad in kimonos carrying fans or brightly coloured woodblock prints of Mount Fuji and pretty temples in the snow, which were freely circulating in Europe during the 1880s. They would certainly have read Isabella Bird's *Unbeaten Tracks in Japan* and been thrilled, even alarmed, at some of her adventures in those parts of the country rarely visited by foreigners. Had the young women seen Gilbert and Sullivan's light opera *Mikado*, first performed in 1885, their impressions of Japan would have been both comic and warped.

While Japan was undoubtedly exotic, it was, from the missionaries' point of view, a much less dangerous and diseased place than most in their orbit. Moreover, it was a well-established fact that the Japanese were clean, polite, educated, and surely, therefore, impatient to hear what Hannah and her companions were only too eager to tell them.

Closeted on the ship together for over two months, the women had ample opportunity to get to know one another. Grace Nott, small and delicate, made a striking physical contrast to Hannah, but during the passage they formed a friendship that was to prove both fruitful and lasting. Grace obviously relished the voyage and wrote to Crispian Fenn, secretary to the Japan mission in London, expressing enthusiasm over the Christmas services they had attended at the cathedral in Singapore and the two days they had spent in Hong Kong as guests of the bishop.

Hannah, however, found the passage on the whole disagreeable. The missionaries travelled second-class and, as was soon to become abundantly clear to her colleagues, Hannah was not a "second-class" person, preferring to dress expensively and to conduct her affairs with style and panache. A further complication was the presence of her pet dog. Throughout Hannah's long life her dogs were of the utmost importance to her, and setting out on such a journey without one in tow would have been unthinkable. But in a letter to the CMS Hannah did acknowledge that some aspects of the journey were "really enjoyable and there is reason to believe that in the Master's service . . . not altogether fruitless." The latter statement suggests that Hannah had used the opportunity to proselytise among her fellow passengers. Proselytising was a common missionary practice and one watched with fascination by the famous writer Natsume Soseki, who when sailing to England in 1900, observed, "They never fail to make the most of every opportunity that's offered to make converts of us whom they innocently set down as idolaters."[1]

On 16 January 1891, exactly nine weeks after leaving Southampton, the *Denbighshire* docked in Kobe Harbour. Kobe was the last of the treaty ports in Japan to be opened up to foreign commerce and in the view of many contemporary writers the most agreeable. The approach to the harbour was, by all accounts, enchanting. In *Rambles in Japan*, Canon H. B. Tristram had recorded the view as follows: "Islands, bays, terrace-ribbed hills, woods of stately cryptomerias, wooden villages nestling in every recess, the distant ones . . . looking like clumps of mushrooms under the green ridges. Fleets of fishing junks . . . dotted about everywhere, sea birds . . . diving about fearlessly on all sides." The town, seen from the sea, was long and rambling, consisting mostly of low, wooden houses but with a few terraces of stone houses built in the European style in front. To the southeast rose thickly wooded hills and to the north uninterrupted miles of paddy fields.

The weather was fine when the *Denbighshire* dropped anchor, and it is easy to imagine the five missionaries gathered up on deck, anxious to absorb every new sight and sound before they disembarked. No record survives of Hannah's emotions as she watched the novel scene unfold before her, whether she was thrilled by what she saw or just plain homesick. But one thing is certain: Hannah had in every sense travelled a very long way from Barnet in Hertfordshire and the militia barracks where she had been born on 17 October 1855.

2

Beginnings

Barnet is now an indistinguishable part of north London but in Hannah's day it was little more than a large village. The pleasant surrounding countryside was filled with market gardens busy supplying the capital lying only a few miles away. The people who lived in Barnet were a rich social mix, ranging from minor aristocracy to farm labourers.

At the time of Hannah's birth her parents were already in their forties, both having been married before, with three children between them. In later years most of Hannah's Japanese friends would assume that she was of noble ancestry but this was far from the truth, her family roots being essentially working class.

Her father, Daniel, who all his life spelled his name the less fashionable way Riddle, was born in 1810 into a large and impoverished Scottish family in Glasgow. For a time he tried to follow his father's occupation of hand-weaving. But with the introduction of mechanical looms, demand for this skill was in decline, and as soon as he was old enough, young Daniel followed in his older brother's footsteps by joining up with the 26th Regiment of Foot, the Cameronians.

On 1 January 1829 he signed up with the army for a period of seven years, receiving a bounty of two pounds, eight shillings, and sixpence, a large sum for someone in his circumstances. Almost immediately he was despatched to India, where the main body of the regiment was stationed. In India he served seven years with little distinction, remaining a private all that time although he might easily have been promoted to corporal had he performed well. His army record describes him as being 5 feet 8 $\frac{1}{2}$ inches tall—it was not from her father that Hannah inherited her unusual height—with a fresh complexion, light brown hair, and blue-grey eyes. His character was noted as "unexceptional."

The army which Daniel Riddle joined was not popular with the general public, who regarded the Royal Navy as the real protector of the country. The officers were poorly trained and the soldiers described by E. M. Spiers in *Army and Society* as "the sweepings of the cities." The Duke of Wellington, the dominant influence on the British army in the first half of the nineteenth century, harboured few illusions about his men:

> People talk of their enlisting for their fine military feeling—all stuff, no such thing. Some of our men enlist for having got bastard children, some for minor offences, many more for drink; but you can hardly conceive such a set brought together and it really is wonderful that we should have made them the fine fellows they are.[1]

It is likely that Daniel himself fathered an illegitimate son. In 1829 a boy called Daniel Riddle was born, whose father, also Daniel Riddle, was described as a "soldier deceased"[2] and whose birth fit in neatly with our Daniel's pre-embarkation leave.

Daniel's initial army career may have lacked distinction but he did well merely to stay alive. During the period he served in India, a far greater number of soldiers died from diseases such as cholera, malaria, and dysentery than from military action. The annual rate of mortality amongst the European troops in India during the time Daniel was there was no less than sixty-nine per thousand.[3] That many soldiers took comfort in the bottle is hardly surprising, and Daniel seems to have gone through a bad period in 1835, when he was disciplined three times for drunkenness.

At the end of his seven years Daniel was offered the opportunity to sign up for a further spell of military service but decided instead to head for home. Once back in Scotland, however, he found economic circumstances little changed and prospects for employment as unpromising as they had been seven years earlier. It was only a matter of months before he was trying to re-enlist, and on 23 October 1837 he rejoined the army on a full-career engagement with the Cameronians, receiving this time a bounty of nine pounds.

The army was obviously glad to take Daniel back. He was swiftly promoted to corporal and, less than a year later, to sergeant. In 1839 he wedded Anne Sawfield but had little time to enjoy married life. In December 1840 he left England as the only sergeant in a detachment of three officers, two corporals, 439 privates, twelve women, and six children on a six-month voyage out to China. One of the young ensigns was Horatio de Quincey, son of the writer Thomas de Quincey, who had concluded that the only way to settle the family's appalling debts was to buy a commission for his son and send him off to the lucrative East. It was a tragic investment. Horatio died of fever only two months after arriving in Hong Kong, as did Daniel's brother, Archibald, a few weeks later.

The regiment fought well in China, but deaths from disease continued unabated—128 in three months.[4] To make matters worse, almost as many men were lost in accidents such as drowning as were killed in action. After a few months the regiment withdrew to India and then returned to England. Daniel spent a further seven years with the Cameronians, dealing with civil disturbances caused by industrial unrest and the potato famine but never again went overseas. His health had been permanently damaged in the East and in 1850, suffering from hepatitis, he was given a medical discharge and a pension of two shillings a day.

Daniel tried living in Glasgow for a couple of years but for whatever reason was drawn back south and in 1853 enlisted in the militia, a part-time volunteer force administered by the lord lieutenants of counties and liable only for home service. At the time Daniel became a member of the permanent staff, the militia was rapidly expanding partly due to fears of revolution and partly because of heavy losses in the Crimean War (1853–56). Daniel was tasked with commissioning a new unit at Barnet. While the barracks were being built he was temporarily lodged at Enfield, where on 5 August 1854, in the Independent Chapel, Daniel, by then a widower, married Hannah Wright, a widow.

Thanks to immaculate army records, it is possible to piece together something of Daniel's life and movements, but unfortunately almost nothing is known of his second wife, Hannah. Her maiden name was Hunt, and she was born in 1814 in the Kent village of Meopham, the daughter of a farm labourer. At some point the family moved to St. Albans, where in February 1843 she wedded Samuel Wright, also a labourer, in what was to be a pathetically short marriage. The following November Samuel died of pneumonia, and three days later, in the charitable City of London Lying-In Hospital, Hannah gave birth to a baby boy. There is no record of how she managed to support herself and her young son, Samuel, during the next ten years until she met and married Daniel. Possibly she went to live with her family in St. Albans, a move that would have put her in the right part of England to meet her future husband.

As soon as the barracks at Barnet were completed, Daniel, his new wife, and their respective children were able to move in to their official accommodation, No. 9, The Barracks, which was where Hannah was born on 17 October 1855. Daniel was primarily a staff instructor in drill and musketry, but his duties also included visiting neighbouring units and chasing up absentees. His busiest time was during annual training, which lasted for a month in September or October after the harvest and which culminated in an exercise, parade, or display. But for most of the year, life as a staff sergeant was undemanding, and the couple was able to supplement Daniel's army pension and militia pay of one shilling and sixpence a day by running a shop in Barnet High Street.

Of Hannah's childhood we know nothing except that following in her father's faith she was christened in the Congregationalist Chapel in Barnet. Her mother, however, belonged to the Church of England and no doubt on occasions took her small daughter (despite her non-conformist baptism) to services at the local Anglican church, Christ Church. Both the vicar, William Pennefather, and his wife, Catherine, were closely associated with missionary work, and their vicarage was noted as a place where noblemen, farmers, bishops, and non-conformist ministers could meet and debate on equal terms. It is tempting to believe that it was under their roof that Hannah first learned of missionary work.

Hannah's subsequent career suggests that she received a sound education. Her parents were relatively affluent, and with their older children grown-up, they may well have decided that the best investment they could make for their young daughter was in her education. As a child, Hannah must have been stirred by her father's stories of India. She grew up with soldiers' tales and was familiar with the trappings of the military, which may account for the obvious pleasure she took from teaching young men and soldiers in her missionary career.

Daniel's health did not improve. In 1871 he was finally discharged from the militia, medically unfit. All things considered, Daniel and the army had served each other well. He had given nearly forty years of his life to military service, but in return he had achieved a social status and prestige that would have eluded him had he remained an unemployed weaver in Scotland.

Any hopes Daniel nurtured of settling down to a comfortable and peaceful retirement were overturned by a family tragedy. On 1 January 1872, in grotesque imitation of his own father's death, Samuel Wright, Hannah's half-brother, died of pneumonia at the age of twenty-eight, leaving a widow and two small children, Samuel, aged four, and Ada Hannah, aged two. Employed variously as a warder, a postal worker, and, at the time of his death, a brewery servant, Samuel had married a local girl, Miranda Neades, the daughter of a master gardener. But after her husband's premature death Miranda seems to have vanished completely. In later years Ada recorded in her diary the date of her father's death but never once mentioned her mother. What happened to Miranda remains a mystery but soon after Samuel's death his children moved into their grandmother's home. At a tender age, therefore, Hannah found herself a surrogate mother, a role that does much to explain the extraordinarily close relationship that developed between her and her niece, Ada, one which was to endure all their lives.

3

Bankrupt

In 1877 the Riddell family went to live in Oystermouth, a village in south Wales some six miles west of Swansea and part of a district known as Mumbles. The reasons for this move are not difficult to guess. Daniel was in poor condition physically, and Mumbles was thought to be a bracing and healthy place to live. And having lived close to London for so long, the Riddells need not have feared rural isolation. Oystermouth was conveniently linked to the rapidly developing town of Swansea by a railroad famous for having carried the very first passenger trains in the world.

But there was another important consideration. With parents who were already elderly and with a young nephew and niece who needed feeding and educating, Hannah, although little more than a girl herself, became the family's chief breadwinner. For Victorian women the choice of work was limited, and for an upwardly mobile young woman like Hannah there was, in reality, only one option—teaching. If Hannah ran her own school, she could not only support the family but also provide them with a home. In 1877 she took the bold step of leasing Russell House in Oystermouth, and on 13 July of that year the following advertisement appeared in the *Cambrian*, a local newspaper:

Russell House, Castleton, Mumbles.
PREPARATORY BOARDING and DAY SCHOOL for Young Gentlemen conducted by Mrs. and Miss Riddell. Young Ladies are received as day

pupils. The House is beautifully and healthily situated in view of the Sea, and close to the ruins of Oystermouth Castle. Special attention paid to the Home comforts and training of the pupils. There are separate school rooms. The ensuing quarter will commence JULY 25th.

By 1877 there were already many small private boarding schools in the Mumbles area. These had burgeoned as a result of the rapidly growing numbers of professional people working in nearby Swansea seeking a good education for their children. Thistleboon House was the most distinguished of the local schools, and young Samuel Wright was sent there. Although money must have been tight in the Riddell household, it is not a surprise to discover Samuel attending the finest school in the area. Throughout her life, despite many financial ups and downs, Hannah rarely compromised her instinct to go for the best.

How much success Hannah achieved with her school is difficult to judge but it is possible to track its progress through the advertisements that appeared regularly in the *Cambrian* until the school was closed in 1889. The idea of taking "Young Gentlemen" as boarders must have quickly faded because in 1879 Russell House was being advertised as an educational establishment for "Young Ladies," with a resident French governess and vacancies for three boarders. German was later added to the curriculum.

On the night of the 1881 census there were six pupils boarding in Russell House, as well as an assistant teacher, a German girl (presumably also a teacher), and two servants. A surprising omission from the census is Ada, but perhaps it had been decided that she, like her brother, should be educated away from home.

With the school established and apparently prospering, life in Oystermouth for the Riddells should have been agreeable. The village was pleasant and Russell House (now a Chinese take-away restaurant) was in an excellent location at the end of a terrace, with views of the Bristol Channel and the castle ruins. There were shops conveniently close and the railway station was only a few minutes' walk away. Furthermore, the Riddells were living in a growing and successful community. Mumbles had iron ore, tourism, a flourishing oyster trade, and its proximity to Swansea made it a tempting location for professional people who had to work in the city but preferred to live in surroundings with a higher social cachet.

Both Daniel and his wife were devout but in Oystermouth they worshipped at different ends of the religious spectrum. Daniel, a non-conformist all his life, was the senior deacon at the Congregationalist Chapel, immediately across the street from Russell House. His wife, on the other hand, was Church of England and went to services at All Saints, a church which belonged to the High tradition of John Newman and Edward Pusey. Perhaps at this stage in her life Hannah accompanied her parents to both churches but later, by choosing to join the CMS, she made clear her preference for Low Church orthodoxy.

By the beginning of 1885 the school had expanded its offerings to art, piano, harp, violin, singing, gymnastics, calisthenics, and mathematics and was able to boast that numerous certificates had been obtained in competitive examinations. Music was something of a speciality, as this enthusiastic coverage of the annual Russell House concert by the *Mumbles Chronicle* of 22 December 1888 makes clear:

> There was a large and influential attendance, the elite of the neighbourhood being present and also several Swanseaites. The programme was an elaborate and attractive one, and was gone through in a manner as to reflect considerable credit on one and all and speaks well for the promoters of the concert, which was a decided success both from a musical and financial point of view.

The concert might have been a success—the proceeds of eight pounds were used to buy Christmas presents for the poor of the parish—but behind the scenes all was far from well. Hannah's mother, who was quoted in the advertisements as co-principal, had died of liver cancer two years earlier, and her illness and death increased Hannah's burdens both physically and emotionally. In 1886 Hannah began to advertise almost weekly in the *Cambrian*, which suggests that it was during this period that the school began to fail. To make matters worse, a few doors up the street a rival establishment was opened by the Misses Potts, who smugly proclaimed in their advertisement in the *Cambrian* that they were the daughters of a clergyman.

Daniel Riddle died on 8 March 1889, as the *Mumbles Chronicle* put it, "after a long and painful illness borne with great Christian patience." It must have been a grim time for Hannah trying simultaneously to nurse her sick father and run the school on dwindling resources. Daniel's death also meant the end of his army pension, a fact that can hardly have helped Hannah's financial problems. Indeed, these troubles proved insurmountable, and in the same month that her father died, Hannah was declared bankrupt.

During this harrowing period Hannah sought help from her half-sister, Isabella Huygens. We know of the latter's existence only because of two letters which turned up in the Lambeth Palace Archive which reveal how dire Hannah's situation had become. Her affairs were already in the hands of the receiver and she was about to go through the bankruptcy court when her brother-in-law lent her his savings of 227 pounds. Eight years later Isabella lobbied the Archbishop of Canterbury in an attempt to retrieve the money from Hannah, who was, by then, already a missionary with the CMS in Japan.

The CMS took the matter very seriously and made a thorough investigation of the circumstances surrounding this family row. Finally they accepted a statement from Hannah's solicitor that the money she received from her sister and brother-in-law had been given on the understanding that it would be repaid only if Hannah's fortunes improved at some future date. Whatever the rights and wrongs of the situation, the incident is a good illustration of the precarious financial tightrope that Hannah trod most of her life.

The last advertisement for Russell House appeared in the *Cambrian* on 3 May 1889. On 29 June the *Chronicle* reported that Hannah had been released as a bankrupt, despite a strong plea from the official receiver that she had failed to keep proper accounts and had contracted debts without having any reasonable hope of paying them.

CHAPTER 4

Liverpool

Hannah was thirty-four years old and penniless, but at least her responsibilities were fewer. Her parents were dead and young Samuel, at twenty-one, was independent. But there was still Ada. Hannah was ambitious for her niece and had somehow managed to find the resources to send her to a finishing school in Switzerland. After she closed the school and relinquished the lease of Russell House, Hannah's first priority was to find a means of supporting herself and Ada.

All her life Hannah displayed an instinct for getting to know people of influence. One of her closest friends was the Reverend John Wrenford, a man deeply involved with the YMWCA. His daughter used to sing part-songs with Ada, and quite possibly it was Wrenford who helped Hannah secure her next job as superintendent at the YMWCA in Liverpool.

The gulf between the gentility of life in Mumbles and the poverty of Liverpool was enormous but exactly how much of the latter Hannah actually saw or experienced is not known. The YMWCA where she was employed was situated at No. 10, Great George Square, an elegant eighteenth-century square close to where the cathedral now stands and far removed both physically and spiritually from the squalor of the city's notorious slums. In a wicked world the YMWCA did its best to protect innocent young people while they found their feet and to offer them something resembling a home.

The association undertook to meet any girl on her arrival in Liverpool, advised her not to answer any advertisement, however promising, without consulting some reliable person, and strongly recommended that no teacher or parent should send a girl to Liverpool without contacting the YMWCA first. This was sound advice. Liverpool in the late nineteenth century was a booming port and one of the great metropolises of the British Empire, but it was also the city where "poverty was more desperate, housing more squalid, social distinctions more cruel [and] the state of public health more shocking than elsewhere."[1]

A Unitarian minister who arrived in the city in 1884 described Liverpool in vivid but chilling terms:

> I came to Liverpool . . . knowing only that I was about to take up my residence in the second city of the mightiest Empire the world has ever seen. I admired its public buildings, its vast docks, its stately shipping, its splendid shops, its lovely parks. It seemed to me that this was a city in which one might be proud to be a citizen. But after the first glance I was appalled by . . . the contiguity of immense wealth and abysmal poverty . . . The hordes of ragged and wretched surged up from their native quarters and covered the noblest streets like a flood. Men and women in the cruelest grip of poverty, little children with shoeless feet and bodies pinched . . . swarmed on the very pavements that fronted the most brilliant shops . . . I had seen wealth. I had seen poverty. But never before had I seen the two so jammed together.[2]

The YWCA aimed to provide shop-girls, governesses, teachers, milliners, dressmakers, and "others who have been accustomed to homes in which some measure of refinement has been added to the ordinary home comforts"[3] with accommodation at a modest price together with something of a social life. If a young woman wanted to improve her mind, on returning to No. 10, Great George Square after the day's work, she could attend evening classes in anything from science to scripture to German. By the autumn of 1889 Hannah found herself working in an environment that was similar to that of Russell House. But almost on her doorstep was a world of deprivation very different to any she had previously encountered and of which she could hardly, for long, have been unaware.

During the year that Hannah spent in Liverpool she met Edward Cropper, the man who ten years later was to become the first president of her leprosy hospital. Cropper came from a family of successful Liverpool businessmen distinguished for their philanthropy and devotion to public service. In fact, there were a number of such leading families in Liverpool, mostly non-conformist, whose members' lives were rooted in their religion. But their faith was pragmatic rather than mystical. In their view, financial success equalled obligation to their fellow human beings, and they embraced these social responsibilities with both zeal and intelligence. Their inspiring example of practical Christianity must have been a telling one for Hannah and may well have contributed to her desire to become a missionary.

Perhaps Hannah took the initiative in approaching The Church Missionary Society or she may have been scooped up in the recruitment drive that followed its decision in 1888 to send single women abroad for the first time. Initially the most eager response to the CMS call came from middle-class spinsters. Of the thirty-one ladies sent abroad by the CMS between 1888 and 1889, nearly half were honorary missionaries who could contribute to their own support and who had probably never before worked for a living.[4] To leave a sheltered and predictable existence in England for an uncertain, even dangerous, one in an alien country required courage. Courage, however, was a quality with which Hannah was amply supplied. For her the CMS represented an opportunity for adventure, achievement, and a new start in life.

The hard-pressed CMS mission in Japan was keen to have its share of the new female work force and in 1890 put in a request for no less than thirteen lady missionaries. They were promised ten but, in fact, received only five, of which Hannah was one.

Putting aside her earlier ambitions to go as a missionary to India, in June 1890 Hannah wrote to the CMS:

> It is with very great pleasure I find from your letter of Saturday morning that Japan is the country thought of as my destination. Had I chosen, I should have desired Japan. I feel very honoured and very grateful to be allowed to enter upon the work and I hope most earnestly that by the aid of the Holy Spirit I may be so guided as to be of real use for the Master, and to the Society.

On 3 October 1890 the following letter was sent to the mission's secretary in Osaka:

My Dear Friend,

We have been able to get five out of the ten ladies for Japan. Let us hope more may still be granted to us.

I have just seen one of them, Miss Riddell*. She is a lady of 33 or 34, who has been in charge of a superior school for the daughters of parents of the wealthier classes. She is <u>willing</u> to take any work, but quite <u>expects</u> (and cheerfully) to be appointed to educational work. The work she <u>likes best</u>, she says, is that of "organising." She has been lately Lady Superintendent of a YMWCA in Liverpool—and she quite understands that it is very possible there may not be scope for that kind of activity on her part for some years to come.

Yours affectionately,
Ch. C. Fenn

*Accent on the second syllable.

Five days later Fenn, secretary to the Japan mission in London, sent Hannah her formal instruction:

The Committee welcome you also, dear Miss Riddell, to their Japan mission. You are desirous to give yourself heartily to the work of making Christ known to the Japanese women. Your past experience has been so ordered in the Providence of God, as to seem clearly to intimate that the educational branch of the work is that to which He has called you. Christ is Lord of all, and therefore of all branches of knowledge; and all that you can teach of God's material creation and of His providential rule of the world can be sanctified to His service and glory. Still your feeling will be, I am determined to know nothing in my teaching, compared with Jesus Christ and Him crucified; and you will not doubt that as in your own individual spiritual life, so also with those that may be your pupils—not this world's learning but Christ crucified will be the power of God and wisdom of God.

On 14 November 1890, five weeks after receiving her formal instruction, Hannah sailed for Japan.

CHAPTER 5

An Exotic New World

Because the steamships arriving at Kobe had to anchor far out from the shore, Hannah and Grace, together with Lizzie Fawcett, Eliza Ritson, and Mary Hunt, were delivered to the dock in a sampan, a ride described by Canon Tristram in *Rambles in Japan* as "much like being tossed around in a tub." The ladies' first encounter with Japanese bureaucracy was at the custom-house, where they were treated with great courtesy and enjoyed their first experience of Japanese good manners, a national habit much remarked on by Western travellers in Meiji Japan.

The welcome party for the new missionaries consisted of Archdeacon Charles Warren, secretary to the Japan mission, and his daughter, together with Katherine Tristram, head of the Bishop Poole School for Girls, and a Miss Hamilton, a teacher in the school. Katherine Tristram, who had known Grace Nott since childhood, was one of the first three lady missionaries employed by the CMS in 1888 and an almost perfect role model for those hoping to follow the missionary calling.

Katherine was the daughter of Canon Tristram of Durham Cathedral, and her pedigree was impeccable. She held a B.A. from London University and had lectured in mathematics at Westfield College before deciding, at the age of twenty-nine, to devote her life to educational missionary work in Japan. Although forceful and effective, she was clearly a woman of great charm and filled with that "culture and good breeding"[1] thought to be such an important quality for female missionaries. Miss Tristram was the first person Hannah Riddell met in Japan, and to Hannah and her comrades so newly arrived in this strange and perplexing land, she must have been a reassuring and familiar figure.

Grace Nott was another excellent example of the kind of woman the CMS liked to recruit. Born in 1863 into a comfortably well-off family, Grace, like Katherine Tristram, came from a very different background from Hannah. By coincidence her father, a captain in the Royal Navy, had played a prominent part in the 1864 action brought by Britain and other Western powers against the Japanese at Shimonoseki, not far from where Grace was to live during her time in Japan. Grace had received part of her education in Germany and had been prepared for missionary work at The Willows, the CMS training college in London. She was exactly the sort of woman the Society wanted—well educated, committed, and financially undemanding:

> The idea of the Society paying the expense of my journey never once entered my head!! Why I should never have dreamt of asking it! My Mother's and my own chief feeling is that we are so very sorry I am <u>obliged</u> to cost the Society any expense at all, and that I cannot at present go out at my own expense! Perhaps in the future God will allow me to have that privilege.[2]

The school of which Miss Tristram was principal traced its origins to 1879, when a Miss Oxlad of the Society for Promoting Female Education in the East opened up her own small house to fourteen pupils, forming one of the earliest private girls' schools in Japan. Indeed, in the 1870s the whole idea of educating girls was a novel one. "The only qualities that befit a woman are gentle obedience, chastity, mercy, and quietness" is a quotation from *The Great Learning for Women*, a famous work based on the Chinese classics and for several centuries the definitive guide to appropriate female behaviour. The book, which is filled with such gems, is popularly attributed to the eminent seventeenth-century moralist Kaibara Ekiken. The author would surely not have approved of the Bishop Poole School for Girls, believing as he did that "a woman should look upon her husband as heaven itself, and never weary of thinking how she may yield to her husband and thus escape celestial castigation."[3]

There were, however, enough families who did welcome the opportunity to educate their daughters that finding adequate space to house the girls had become a problem. In 1886 the annual CMS conference in Japan decided to build a school as a memorial to Bishop Arthur W. Poole, the first Anglican bishop in Japan, who had unfortunately fallen ill on arrival in the country and returned to die in England after only ten months in the job. In his short tenure he had shown great interest in the idea of the fledgling school and had intended to raise funds to find more suitable premises. The object of the school was "to promote vernacular education on Christian principals and, in the case of boarders, to train them in simple domestic duties in the hope that some of them might eventually be selected and prepared for female missionary work."[4]

The new school, completed in March 1890 with funds mostly raised in England, was large enough to house a hundred boarders. It was a handsome red-brick structure with elegant shuttered windows and a fine inner quadrangle. That such an ambitious project should have been realised with the sole object of educating girls must, at the time, have been surprising to many Japanese. To complete the memorial to Bishop Poole, a house adjoining the school had, a few months earlier, been fitted up for female missionaries, and it was here that Mary, Lizzie, and Eliza were lodged, while Hannah and Grace stayed with Katherine Tristram in her house.

The Bishop Poole School for Girls was situated in Osaka in the foreign concession known as Kawaguchi. Concessions were districts assigned to foreigners when the ports were first opened in the late 1850s and were the only parts of the city where foreigners were allowed to hold land. With a population of nearly half a million, Osaka was the second largest city in Japan. But because its harbour was unsuitable for large, modern ocean steamers, Kobe, some twenty-five miles away, became the more important seaport for both cities. Consequently Kawaguchi had been largely abandoned by merchants, and by 1891 the fine, spacious houses they had left behind were occupied by foreigners, most of whom were associated with missionary bodies.

When Hannah and Grace were taken sightseeing by Katherine Tristram during their first few days in Osaka, they were shown the great castle with its magnificent curving wall built of huge stones fitted together without mortar. This formidable fortress, built in the sixteenth century, housed a massive arsenal, and as it was the headquarters of one of the six military divisions, was home to a large garrison. The picturesque wooden keep, or donjon, had long since been destroyed by fire, but from high up on the surviving ramparts the newcomers could look out over Osaka and see many of its six hundred bridges and canals and the numerous tall factory chimneys that had sprouted in recent years. The women were told how missionary work was being conducted in the cotton mills and match factories, and they learned about Osaka's other flourishing industries, the timber and shipbuilding yards, the ironworks, and the mint.

Miss Minna Tapson, a missionary who had travelled out to Osaka with Miss Tristram in 1888, described some of their strange new experiences in an article published in the *Church Missionary Gleaner* the following year:

> Osaka is a city of bridges. This was our first impression of it. As the streets all look exactly like one another, and have no names—or if they have we cannot read them, as they are in Chinese characters—we hoped the bridges would act as landmarks, but as they too are just alike, and occur in the most unexpected places, they only confuse one rather more. The streets are very narrow, but as the jinrikishas are the only conveyances ever seen here, they are wide enough, excepting on festive occasions, when everybody, including the matrons with their blackened teeth and their babies on their backs, play battledore and shuttlecock across the main streets. At least this has been going on during the New Year festivities, when the houses are nearly all decorated with wreaths of evergreens and chrysanthemums, and over the doorways an arrangement of ferns and oranges, and sometimes lobsters. It is the fashion on New Year's Day for the ladies to stay at home and the gentlemen to pay calls. We had a good number of callers, but as scarcely any of them could speak any English, and we could speak no Japanese, the calls were very silent, and rather embarrassing and we still feel inclined to laugh at ourselves when we make our profound bows, with our hands placed on our knees, in true Japanese style.

Among the first Buddhist temples Hannah visited was Tennoji in Osaka. There, in a fine park, stood a temple dedicated to deceased children, where hundreds of items of infant clothing hung as offerings to Buddha from bereaved parents. In exchange for a small payment, the wretched mother would receive a sliver of wood on which was inscribed the dead child's name and which she would cast into a pool just at the point where water poured from a giant stone tortoise's mouth. If she was lucky, the wood became instantly soaked, thus ensuring her child an easy passage in the journey after death.[5] Exposed for the first time to such "heathen" practices, Hannah, with her characteristic energy and need for action, must have felt some impatience to begin preaching the Christian message of salvation to a people she could see were so clearly in need of it.

Osaka was the headquarters of the CMS in central Japan. By the time Hannah arrived there, the society had a variety of flourishing institutions, including several churches and schools, a facility for training "Bible women," and a divinity college for instructing Japanese clergy. Minna Tapson described the missionaries' world in an article in the *Church Missionary Gleaner*:

> There are two CMS churches in Osaka, and there is one Native clergyman . . . We enjoy hearing him preach so much, not that we can understand a word that he says, of course . . . His wife is a charming little woman and speaks English beautifully . . . Even in the towns the presence of an English woman acts as an attraction to a meeting—in the country places it will ensure a large congregation . . . It seems just as desirable and necessary here as it is at home, if a healthy Church life is to be sustained, to give its members something to do and as the Japanese are particularly fond of hearing themselves speak in public, it is the more desirable to give them the right thing to talk about . . . When I was at home we heard about "open doors in Japan"; here it seems as if we could see them opening all round us, disclosing endless opportunities, and suggesting infinite possibilities. And <u>how</u> we long to enter in and take possession in His name! Meanwhile we have need of patience.

A fair proportion of the forty CMS missionaries (including wives) recorded as working in Japan in 1891 were living in Osaka. The five new ladies were therefore immediately taken into the bosom of a small but well-organised band of fellow travellers, which must have helped counter some of the strangeness of their new environment.

The longest serving missionary in Osaka at the time was the Reverend Charles Warren, who with his flowing white beard looks in photographs every inch the venerable archdeacon that he was. Whereas The Society for the Propagation of the Gospel (SPG) missionaries tended to be drawn from the well-off, middle classes of English society and educated at

Oxford or Cambridge, most of those in the CMS ranks came from further down the Victorian social scale. Warren was a typical product. His father, a herbalist, also ran a leather shop, and his brothers and brothers-in-law all were tradesmen. His sons, however, who also became missionaries, were Oxford graduates. To a man like Warren, life as a CMS missionary in Japan undoubtedly offered opportunities that were not necessarily available in England at that time. If this was true for a man, it applied even more to a woman of Hannah's modest background.

Warren, the first CMS missionary in central Japan, arrived in 1873 and was joined three years later by the Reverend Henry Evington, who is significant in this story because he crossed swords so strikingly with Hannah a few years later. The world of British missionaries in Japan was a small one, and it is thus not surprising—indeed is even rather touching—to find Archdeacon Warren, a widower, marrying one of Hannah's shipmates, Lizzie Fawcett, only sixteen months after her arrival.

The challenges confronting Hannah and her Protestant colleagues in the 1890s may have seemed formidable. But compared with those that had faced their Catholic missionary forbears some 250 years earlier, their road ahead was remarkably smooth.

6

Christian Pioneers

When Francis Xavier first brought Christianity to Japan in 1549, he achieved considerable success, although he was in the country only twenty-seven months. Within a few years, a number of daimyo, or feudal lords, and other men of high rank had been converted, and by 1580 it was reckoned that there were about 150,000 Christians in the country. But this fair wind was not to persist. Suspicion grew that the Jesuit missions existed to disguise plans for Western political domination, and the tide began to turn against Christianity.

A number of factors contributed to this change of attitude. In Kyushu the Christians were growing strong enough to pose a threat to a new and fragile political stability, or so it seemed to Toyotomi Hideyoshi, the second of the three great leaders who ruled Japan from 1568 to 1616. Although it was never proven, Hideyoshi also believed that Portuguese merchants were buying Japanese criminals and taking them as slaves to India.[1] He must have also absorbed much of the propaganda put out by Buddhist priests, who naturally regarded Christianity as a hostile rival to their own faith.

In 1587 Hideyoshi published an edict expelling the Jesuits but it was not until his successor, Tokugawa Ieyasu, issued a decree banning Christianity in 1614 that it was effectively extinguished. Notices were put up in every town and village prohibiting the "evil sect of Christianity" and offering rewards for the discovery of priests or converts. One of the most successful methods of rooting out closet Christians was to make suspects trample on a cross or a picture of Christ. Within a few years all the missionaries had been killed or expelled. Despite this remorseless persecution, a number of Japanese Christians, mostly around Nagasaki, hung on to their faith, keeping it a secret from the outside world.

In 1639 the Tokugawa government extended its expulsion order on missionaries to include all foreigners, and with the exception of a handful of Dutch traders confined to Deshima, a tiny island off Nagasaki, Japan settled down to a period of over two hundred years of isolation and introspection, virtually cut off from all foreign influences. It was a period of remarkable and novel stability during which the country was free from civil war and foreign designs.

During this time foreigners did try to influence Japanese affairs but were unsuccessful. With the development of the west coast of America, US interest in the Pacific was greatly increased, but various attempts to prise open Japan during the 1840s were fruitless. Eventually, in July 1853, Commodore Matthew C. Perry anchored off Yokohama with a squadron of four ships and effectively delivered an ultimatum demanding that the Japanese government make arrangements for supplying American ships, look after shipwrecked sailors, and, most importantly, open formal relations with the United States.

Such uncompromising overtures threw the shogunate government into confusion and disarray. The shogunate was forced to recognise its own weakness in the face of possible Western aggression and to acknowledge the awful likelihood of the colonisation of Japan by Western powers if it did not make some concessions. While the shogunate may have done its best to cut itself off from all foreign influence, it was certainly aware of the colonial fate that had befallen a number of other Asian countries. As a result, despite much passionate opposition, the shogunate arrived at a "Treaty of Friendship" with the Americans. Thereafter, a number of agreements were signed during the 1850s with other unwelcome and pushy nations, including Britain, Russia, France, Prussia, and Holland. Officially styled as treaties of amity and commerce, they were popularly called the "unequal treaties" because, although Westerners were allowed to reside only in selected cities—Hakodate, Yokohama, Kobe, Osaka, Nagasaki, Niigata, and Tokyo—they were almost completely removed from Japanese control. The foreigners were subject only to their own laws and even had sole responsibility for setting the tariffs on foreign imports to Japan.

The energetic Townsend Harris, the first American Consul and a keen Christian, ensured that the Japanese agreed to Americans having the right to "the free exercise of their religion" and "the right to erect suitable places of worship." The United States government undertook to promise that its citizens in Japan would do nothing to stir up religious enmity, while in their turn the Japanese gave assurance that the trampling on religious emblems had been already abolished.[2]

With these ground rules established, Christian clergy began once more to enter the country. On 2 May 1859 the Reverend John Liggins of the Protestant Episcopal Church of America became the first undisguised missionary to set foot in Japan since the unfortunate Father Giovanni Battista Sidotti, who had died in captivity 150 years earlier. Other missionaries soon followed but, despite this slight melting of the perma-frost, to most Japanese, who for the last couple of centuries had been told only of the evils of Christianity, the religion continued to be a total anathema. Indeed, Christianity remained illegal until 1873, and, al-though largely ignored, the notices banning Christianity still stood in every village and town.

In 1868 the weakened and ineffective shogunate finally succumbed to imperial forces, and Emperor Meiji moved from Kyoto to Tokyo to take up his role as head of state, his ancient rights fully restored. During the 1860s anti-foreign sentiment was often intense, and one of the first actions of the new imperial government was to issue instructions to the Kyushu authorities to arrest and deport all Christians living in the Nagasaki area. Three thousand were rounded up and exiled to the north of the country despite strong protests by the representatives of the West-ern powers. The Japanese stood their ground, maintaining their right to do what they liked outside the treaty ports and accusing the Japanese Christians of insulting behaviour at Shinto shrines. At the same time missionaries continued to be denied permission to travel in rural Japan without special permits, which were difficult to obtain.

The Japanese government was in an unenviable position. On the one hand, the government detested its subordinate position to the foreigners and understandably wished to re-negotiate the unequal treaties as soon as possible. On the other hand, some Japanese in positions of power were beginning to recognise that Japan would never be able to stand shoulder to shoulder with the West and thus regain complete independence without absorbing Western technology and achieving Western educational, legal, medical, and military standards.

A turning point in attitudes to the West occurred in 1873. In that year members of a Japanese embassy (the Iwakura mission) that had travelled to America and Europe in 1871 to negotiate revision of the treaties returned to Japan chastened by what they now realised was a much bigger gap between the West and Japan than they had previously anticipated. On their return, a comprehensive programme of what would these days be described as a major restructuring was launched and, after nearly 250 years, Christianity once more became legal.

As the Japanese began to welcome rather than shun things Western, Christianity emerged as a beneficiary of the new mood. Throughout the remainder of the seventies and most of the eighties, Christians were optimistic about their progress, and many felt that it was only a matter of time and hard work before the whole country became converted to Christ. The optimism was premature. Shortly before Hannah arrived in Japan, an obvious reaction to earlier enthusiasm for the West had begun to be evident. The *Japan Weekly Mail* of 27 April 1889 doubtless reflected the view of many Japanese when it expressed concern lest the country lose its individuality and declared its growing conviction "that the way to compete with foreign countries was not to follow in their wake by copying their example but rather to strengthen and develop the faculties that belong especially to the genius of the country."[3]

Just as Christianity had earlier benefited from its clear association with such aspects of Western learning as medicine and education, it now suffered from the hostility shown to the very foreign influences so recently and enthusiastically embraced. Anti-Christian editorials appeared in influential newspapers, suggesting "Christianity will destroy patriotism, filial duty, and loyalty to the Mikado, give rise to religious wars, and become the secret means of foreign interference."[4]

But there were other reasons why Christianity was not prospering when Hannah and her companions arrived in 1891. In that year there were some thirty different Protestant missions operating in Japan, not to mention the Roman Catholic and the Russian Orthodox ones. The sheer number of different denominations must have been deeply perplexing to the Japanese. The missionaries did at least all acknowledge Christ as the supreme Master but each mission claimed its own brand of Christianity was the real one. An amusing instance of interdenominational rivalry recorded in the *History of the CMS* concerned the famous missionary the Reverend John Batchelor, who was engaged in converting the Ainu in Hokkaido. His relative success attracted the attention of the Roman Catholics, who, according to the possibly less than totally objective CMS report, swiftly moved into his territory, claiming that as his name signified an unmarried man, he had no right to have a wife!

One measure of comfort to Western missionaries at this time was the fact that the president of the brand-new national parliament, opened in 1890, was a Christian, as indeed were eleven of its new members. One correspondent to the *Church Missionary Society Intelligencer* compared the stir caused by the elections to the "interest of children in a new romp [which] seems for the time to have diverted some amount of public attention from the subject of religion."

CHAPTER 7

The Language

The young women, fresh out from England, immediately faced many tests, not least of them the Japanese language. On the matter of language the CMS was very clear: for a missionary to be effective he or she had to have a good grasp of the vernacular, and every missionary was required to take well-organised and stringent examinations over a period of several years.

Hannah was clearly eager to begin her study of Japanese. In a letter to the CMS secretary for Japan, Crispian Fenn, just before she left England, she thanked him for sending her the *Grammar of the Vernacular* and expressed regret that she was not to have use of a dictionary on the voyage out but understood that "the Society <u>must</u> consider the cost of books supplied to so many." On arrival in Osaka, the women soon got down to work. In a letter to the CMS, Grace Nott wrote, "We were not able to begin study till February 1st but from that time till we left Osaka, I studied with Mori-san and one of the elder girls from the school. Also for a short time I had another teacher for reading."

It is unlikely that many missionaries, so full of enthusiasm for the task ahead, realised before they reached the country just how difficult even rudimentary Japanese is to learn. An American missionary, M. L. Gordon, described the problem in *An American Missionary in Japan:* "He [the missionary] has doubtless been encouraged to regard this obstacle as of a very temporary character, and he indulges in the pleasing hope that a few weeks, or a few months at the farthest, will find him speaking like a native." The reality was very different. Even Katherine Tristram, herself a highly intelligent woman who deeply loved Japan and spent a total of fifty years there, never managed to achieve fluency in the language. Although this seems scarcely credible, the following passage from *An American Missionary in Japan* describes the unfortunate foreigner's plight:

> When he reaches his destination, however, his complacency receives a terrible shock. Geographically speaking, he is near the people whom he hopes to teach; but as far as actual teaching is concerned, a broader ocean than the Pacific still rolls between him and them. As he listens to the shouts of the boatmen who crowd around his ship or the chattering of the jinrikisha men while they draw lots for the privilege of carrying him to his hotel, he understands as never before, why the Russians call foreigners "the dumb," "the speechless," and say even of modern English travelers, "Look at these people! They make a noise but cannot speak."

The wretched missionary, having discovered the unexpected difficulties in accomplishing even the simplest of communications let alone preaching the gospel, had, according to Dr. Gordon, several options open to him. He could, for instance, confine himself to the small but increasing number of Japanese who spoke English. Or he could try using an interpreter, sometimes only half jokingly described as an "interrupter." Perhaps he could specialise, like the American theological student who felt that he had a particular calling to "labor among educated young ladies."[1] Or being of a dramatic bent, he might emulate the Scottish missionary in China who, even before he reached his destination, attempted to teach the doctrine of the atonement to the boatmen who came alongside the ship by going through the motions of washing a garment.[2]

Of the dictionaries available to late nineteenth-century students of Japanese, the standard work was by Dr. James Hepburn, who came to Japan as one of the first medical missionaries in the late 1850s and quickly achieved success as a doctor. But it is for his work as a scholar of the Japanese language that Hepburn is chiefly remembered, especially for the dictionary over which he laboured for thirteen years. The inveterate traveller Isabella Bird, who was in Japan in 1878, stayed with Dr. Hepburn in Yokohama and described him as being "by no means enthusiastic about the Japanese, or sanguine regarding their future in any respect, and evidently thinks them deficient in solidity."[3]

Books are not much use without teachers and, as Dr. Gordon pointed out in *An American Missionary in Japan*, if the missionary managed to find himself a teacher who understood English, he would find himself talking in English <u>about</u> the Japanese language, learning something of the science of the language, but making little progress in the art of speaking it. On the other hand, if he employed a teacher who knew no English, the two of them would sit in a room together with no means of communication except signs and a Japanese-English dictionary.

Having at last acquired both teacher and books, the reasonably intelligent missionary should have found his studies plain sailing but, as Dr. Gordon wrote, this was not the case:

> Our Friend begins in a concrete way by inquiring the names of the most familiar things about the house, using the one sentence given him by an older missionary, *Kore wa nani to moshimasu ka?* (What is this?). In answer to this question he is told that the rice on the table is called *meshi*. Rejoicing in this knowledge, he begins making sentences like "I eat *meshi*" and "the child likes *meshi*." "No," says his mentor. "In speaking of a child's rice, it is better to use the word *mama*, as in "the child likes *mama*." Undiscouraged, the student tries again with "Do you eat *meshi*?" when his teacher stops him, and tells him that it is polite, in speaking to another of his having or eating rice, to call it *gozen*. Having taken this in, he goes on with his sentence-building with "the merchant sells *gozen*," when the teacher again calls a halt, and tells him that *meshi* and *gozen* are used for cooked rice only, and that for unboiled rice *kome* is the proper word. Feeling that he is now getting into the secrets of language, he says, "*kome* grows in the fields," when he is again stopped with the information that growing rice is called *ine!*

Eugene Stock, the CMS historian, quoted some opinions about the Japanese language formed by lady missionaries whom, he claims, were usually good at linguistic studies. A Miss Johnson wrote that Japanese was "simply and absolutely appalling," while a Miss Cockram called it "beautiful and baffling," and a Miss Allen described it as "very fascinating and illustrating in many ways the character of the people."[4]

But Hannah was occupied with many matters apart from struggles with the language during her first two months in Japan. She was instinctively a political animal and would have lost no time in immersing herself in the complexities of recent Japanese history and studying the nascent political structures that were emerging around the time she first arrived in the country. Her chief concern would have been to understand Japanese politics and history in relation to Christianity and to grasp how that knowledge might be useful in bringing about the conversion of the whole country to the Christian faith. Indeed, many of her contemporary missionaries seriously thought that such a conversion could be accomplished by the turn of the century.

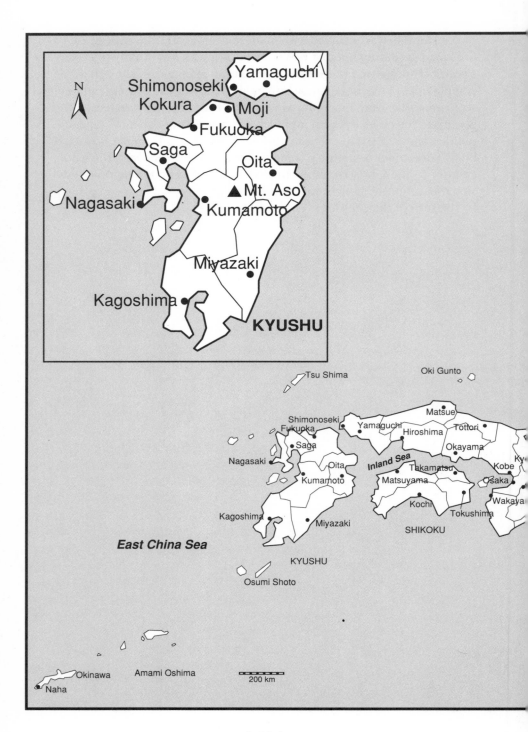

KYUSHU

East China Sea

Tsu Shima

Oki Gunto

Matsue

Shimonoseki
Fukuoka
Yamaguchi
Hiroshima
Tottori

Saga
Okayama

Nagasaki
Oita
Inland Sea
Takamatsu
Kobe
Ky

Kumamoto
Matsuyama
Osaka

Kagoshima
Kochi
Tokushima
Wakaya

Miyazaki
SHIKOKU

KYUSHU

Osumi Shoto

Okinawa
Amami Oshima
200 km

Naha

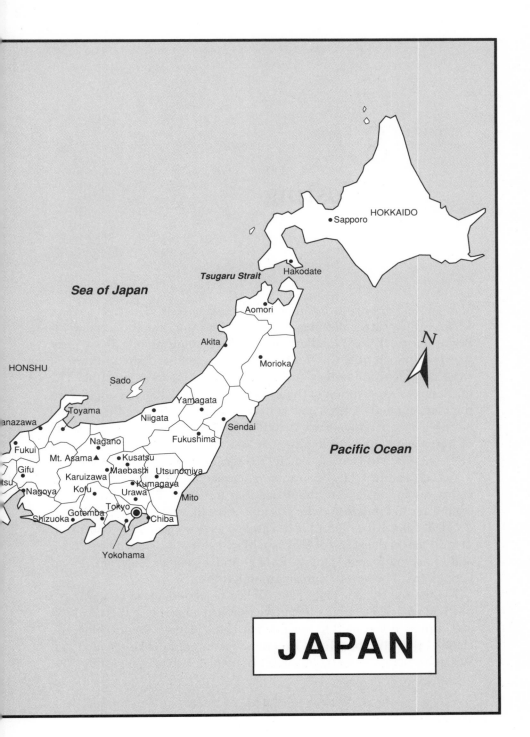

8

Posting

Hannah had arrived in Japan at an interesting time. The first wave of Meiji enthusiasm for all things Western was waning, and the country was beginning to flex its intellectual muscle. Having absorbed—at great speed—so much from the West, many Japanese now desired to turn all these new ideas and systems into a recognisably Japanese structure. The missionaries' observation of these energetic and intelligent people, with their ancient and sophisticated culture, led them to believe that it could be only a matter of time, increased effort, and manpower before the whole of Japan was converted to Christendom. In other words, the Japan of 1891 presented to Hannah exactly the sort of challenge she relished.

In that year the CMS Japan conference met on 1 April in Osaka. Some eighty resolutions and recommendations were sent back to the parent committee in London and the postings of the new recruits from England decided. Eliza Ritson and Lizzie Fawcett were to go to the mission in Tokushima on the island of Shikoku, Mary Hunt was to remain in Osaka, and Grace Nott and Hannah Riddell and a young clergyman, David Lang, were to be sent to Kumamoto in Kyushu.

Kyushu was the one place Hannah had requested not to be stationed. She had read of a terrible earthquake that had taken place there in 1889 and, although it is hard to imagine her being alarmed by anything, she claimed that the thought of experiencing an earthquake terrified her. Whatever her misgivings, she made no complaint about her posting. The exact date that Hannah and Grace left Osaka is uncertain but it was probably soon after the conference had completed its deliberations.

Hannah and Grace travelled to Kumamoto firstly by steamer from Kobe to Nagasaki through the Inland Sea. This complicated waterway of nearly 250 miles runs between the main island of Honshu and Shikoku on the south. The Inland Sea is dotted with thousands of islands and enchanted many a traveller in Meiji Japan. In 1893 Canon Tristram described it in *Rambles in Japan* as follows:

> We steamed down the Inland Sea, amidst a prospect simply peerless for calm, rich, quiet beauty . . . a silver sea, countless islets on both sides, mountains clad with timber from the shore to their summits, villages in rapid succession, some half buried in woods, others fringing the shore, innumerable fishing-boats and junks, amidst which the steamer carefully threads her way. Not majestic or grand, but delicately, gracefully, sweetly beautiful.

Nagasaki, Hannah and Grace's first stop, was very different from Osaka. The city's streets were narrow and picturesque, with overhanging houses that nearly met in the middle. Even the sampans plying Nagasaki's famous harbour were distinctive, being gondola-shaped with long blue beaks terminating in a red strip and a carrying a curiously shaped cabin. The coaling of the steamships lying at anchor was completed quickly and efficiently by women, some of them with babies strapped to their backs. The women wore huge, limpet-shaped hats made of wilted palm leaves and bright blue and white towels twisted round their hair. Forming a long line that reached from the supply barges up a ladder into the ship's hold, they handed baskets of coal from one to the other, so that a continuous stream poured steadily into the ship.[1] Above the harbour rose pretty green hills dotted with houses. Along the crescent-shaped bund stood the steamship offices, consulates, and banks, and above them the attractive bungalows of the foreign residents built on terraces which were surrounded by camphor laurels, cherry, vegetable-wax, magnolia, orange, and conifers.[2]

Apart from its general attractiveness and long historical links with Christianity, Nagasaki was of special interest to Hannah and Grace because it was the CMS headquarters in Kyushu and the place where the first CMS missionary to Japan, the Reverend George Ensor, landed in

January 1869. At that time Christianity was still illegal and neither public preaching nor teaching was allowed. Although his presence caused a great deal of interest among the local people, only the very brave dared, usually in the dead of night, to find their way to Ensor's house to learn something of the foreigners' religion.

Ensor's house was carefully watched by the Japanese authorities and his life was often in danger. Indeed, his own faithful servant, Futagawa, is alleged to have originally sought his employ with the sole intention of murdering him. Fortunately for Ensor, Futagawa changed his mind and instead became an ardent Christian. He was imprisoned for his faith, yet continued to preach in prison, reportedly with some success, until he was eventually released.[3]

Another anecdote recorded by Ensor himself illustrates his precarious lifestyle. He somehow persuaded the priests of one of the larger Buddhist temples in Nagasaki to let him enter its most inner and holy sanctum, where, as expected, he beheld "the idol, altar, incense, flowers, and all the other paraphernalia of heathen and idolatrous worship." With great bravado—"My heart grew hot within me," he wrote—he proceeded to preach the Christian gospel and inveigh against the "hollowness and fearfulness of idolatry."[4] Ensor survived this encounter and even sparked an interest in debate with the Buddhist priests, but he might just as easily have found himself locked up. At this time in Japan, life for a missionary could still be hazardous, and men like Ensor certainly needed a zealous faith to sustain them in a lonely and stressful existence. But by the time Hannah and Grace reached Nagasaki in April 1891, some eighteen years after Ensor's departure, a church and mission hall had been built and a Christian bookshop was in operation.[5]

The Reverend Albert Fuller was the resident CMS priest in Nagasaki and also the secretary to the Kyushu mission. The latter was an important position because all communication between the missionaries and head-quarters in London had to be channelled through the secretary. Fuller was in Nagasaki to welcome Hannah and Grace, brief them, and help them complete the tiresome formalities involved in acquiring the passport that would allow them to take up residence in Kumamoto. Until 1894, when a new agreement was signed between Britain and Japan (soon to be followed with agreements with other nations), this passport had to be renewed in Nagasaki every three months.

As the crow flies, the distance between Nagasaki and Kumamoto is not great, some fifty miles, but in 1891 there was no direct rail link, and the complicated trip had to be made by train, steamer, and jinrikisha. However uncomfortable the journey, it nevertheless had its compensations. The Japanese countryside in April is ravishing, bursting with cherry blossom, azaleas, and other flowers. The hills are covered with every shade of green imaginable, from the soft lighter shades of feathery bamboo to the sterner dark hues of the cryptomeria trees. The valleys are carpeted with neat, fresh, green paddy fields. The rice, planted in impossibly straight rows, gives a pleasing linear pattern and echoes with the croaking of frogs. Terraces straggle up the lower slopes of the hills, and in Hannah's day farmers were breaking the black soil with ox-driven ploughs. Hannah and Grace could hardly have failed to be captivated by such idyllic scenery. Beside the road they saw small shrines with weather-worn stone statues of the god Jizo adorned with his red bib, and images of Kannon, the all merciful and forgiving deity whose role is to a Christian reminiscent of that of the Virgin Mary.

Hannah, the ardent missionary, travelling across the countryside and seeing such symbols of Japanese faith, must have been stirred by conflicting emotions. Lizzie Fawcett, her erstwhile companion on the *Denbighshire*, posted to Tokushima, expressed the sentiments of many of her fellow missionaries when she wrote the following in a letter to the CMS:

> We arrived in Tokushima about six o'clock and were much struck by the beauty of the place, for it is surrounded by hills on three sides, and everything looked so fresh in the early morning. But in crossing one of the bridges we realised that, in spite of all the beauty which was around us, we were really in a heathen country; for there was a man standing on this bridge praying to the sun, which was just then rising. He was the first we had seen worshipping in this way and it made me feel very sad.

Part of any long journey was made in a jinrikisha, more politely referred to as a *kuruma*. This curious means of transport is said to have been invented in 1869 by an American named Jonathan Goble, who, while living in Yokohama, had the clever notion of converting a pram into a carriage for his invalid wife. The idea caught on with the Japanese, and soon the jinrikisha was to be seen all over Japan. For missionaries, trying to penetrate remote rural areas with their gospel message, it was often the only alternative to walking. Isabella Bird described the *kuruma* in *Unbeaten Tracks in Japan* as follows:

> [It consisted of] a light perambulator body, an adjustable hood of oiled paper, a velvet or cloth lining and cushion, a well for parcels under the seat, two high slim wheels, a pair of shafts connected by a bar at the ends. The body is usually lacquered and decorated according to its owner's taste . . . Some are gaudily painted with contorted dragons, or groups of peonies, hydrangeas, chrysanthemums, and mythical personages . . . The shafts rest on the ground at a steep incline as you get in—it must require much practice to enable one to mount with ease or dignity—the runner lifts them up, gets into them, gives the body a good tilt, and goes off at a smart trot.

For a particularly heavy passenger like Hannah or for someone in a hurry, two men were employed. These jinrikisha pullers were an astonishingly tough breed, and running twenty-five to thirty miles a day over a period of two or three days was considered quite normal. But this mode of travel had its critics, including Lafcadio Hearn, arguably the most eloquent foreign writer in Meiji Japan, writing in *Out of the East:*

> The jolting makes reading too painful; the rattle of the wheels and the rush of the wind render conversation impossible, even when the road allows of a fellow traveller's vehicle running beside your own. And after having become familiar with the characteristics of Japanese scenery, you are not apt to notice during such travel, except at long intervals, anything novel enough to make a strong impression. Most often the way winds through a perpetual sameness of ricefields, vegetable farms, tiny thatched hamlets—and between interminable ranges of green or blue hills.

By whatever means of transport, Hannah and Grace finally reached Kumamoto some time in the second half of April 1891, to be greeted by John Brandram, the resident priest. Brandram, a Cambridge graduate, was thirty-two and had been with the CMS Japan mission since 1884, accompanied by his sister. Initially he had been part of the mission in Nagasaki but since 1887 had been stationed in Kumamoto, the very first CMS missionary to live outside the treaty ports. When Hannah and

Grace arrived, he had been married just one year to his wife, Mary, herself the daughter of a vicar and among the first batch of CMS lady missionaries sent to Japan.

The Brandram ménage lived right in the middle of Kumamoto within a couple of minutes' walk of the remains of the castle. A house had been found for Hannah and Grace in the next street, Choanji-cho, and which Mary Bickersteth, who stayed with them a few months after their arrival, described as being furnished in Japanese fashion and looking very homely. It was the more common practice for missionaries living so far from home and in such a novel and strange environment to try and re-create a little bit of England in their private quarters. The Reverend R. B. Peery, writing in *The Gist of Japan*, had strong views on the subject:

> The mission home should be a Western home transplanted in the East. It may not become too much orientalized. It should have Western furniture, pictures, musical instruments, etc., and should make its possessor feel that he is in a Western home. It should be well supplied with books and newspapers and everything else that will help to keep its inmates in touch with the life of the West. The missionary may not be orientalized, else he will be in danger of becoming heathenized.

Apart from the Brandrams and the new young curate, David Lang, there were no other English people for miles around. Grace Nott was speaking from the heart when in 1891 she wrote in her annual letter to the CMS, "This place does, indeed, make one long to be able to speak . . . long too for more workers, the field is truly large; the thought of a population of 50,000 in the city itself, and almost two millions in Mr. Brandram's district altogether is appalling."

CHAPTER 9

Kumamoto

The city in which the two women found themselves was then the capital of Higo Province and stands on a broad plain encircled by mountains. The smoking crater of a still active volcano, Mount Aso, was visible to the northeast some thirty miles away and a constant reminder to the missionaries that they were living in a land which could erupt, explode, and tremble to devastating effect without warning.

Kumamoto was planted with many trees, and contemporary accounts describe it as having the appearance of a park. A wide river, the Shiraka-wa, winds through the city and in Meiji times was spanned by attractive foot-bridges. This description may sound pleasant enough but Kumamoto was not to everyone's taste. Lafcadio Hearn spent several years in Kumamoto as a teacher and was not impressed:

> A vast, straggling, dull, unsightly town is Kumamoto: there are no quaint, pretty streets, no great temples, no wonderful gardens. Burnt to the ground in the civil war . . . the place still gives you the impression of a wilderness of flimsy shelters erected in haste almost before the soil had ceased to smoke. There are no remarkable places to visit, not, at least, within city limits—no sights—few amusements.[1]

Kumamoto had the reputation of being one of the most conservative cities in Japan. Hearn claimed that it was the least inclined to imitate Western manners and customs, and pointed out that although the samurai were disbanded in 1872, in Kumamoto their code lived on. Laws against extravagance that had been obsolete for a generation still exerted an influence that could be seen in the simple dress and plain direct manners of the people. Hearn wrote that a fierce patriotism and pride in tradition accompanied the conservatism, but did concede that this conservatism was of an idealistic rather than practical nature, noting that the town was not slow in adopting Western technology for agriculture, industry, and the railway.[2]

The outstanding feature of Kumamoto had been the castle. The fifteenth-century structure had been enlarged and rebuilt in 1599 by a celebrated general, Kato Kiyomasa, recognised as Japan's master castle architect. The castle had stood on a rock, precipitous and unassailable on three sides, commanding not only the town but the whole of the surrounding countryside. The roads immediately around the city were sunk deep in the rice fields to enable Kiyomasa to send out secret parties of soldiers from his castle and thus surprise any approaching enemy.[3] Kato Kiyomasa was famously anti-Christian, and if Mount Aso was a reminder of the potential physical dangers facing Hannah and her fellow missionaries, the ruins of Kiyomasa's castle must have been a striking symbol of the spiritual challenges they would confront in their attempts to convert the Japanese to Christianity.

In its original state the castle had no fewer than sixteen towers but during the Satsuma Rebellion of 1877, when disaffected samurai led by a right-wing member of the oligarchy, Saigo Takamori, fought and lost to government forces, it was largely destroyed, and only one of the towers, the ramparts, and a gateway survived. By 1891 the castle was home to the Sixth Division of the Japanese army, newly modelled on the German army.

In *The Cross and the Rising Sun*, A. H. Ion writes that a Kumamoto samurai had been baptised as far back as 1866 but Christianity made its first big impact on the city in 1871 with the arrival of Captain Leroy Janes, an American who came at the invitation of the daimyo of Higo and established a school where foreign subjects were to be taught.[4] Biding his time for several years, Janes first won the confidence of the boys before starting to teach them about Christianity. Years later one of his students wrote, "No pupil could understand English and Captain Janes did not understand the Japanese language, so that the difficulty of communication was extreme"[5]—something of an understatement. But trivialities like these did not deter the captain, who lit such a burning faith in the breasts of some forty of his young students that one beautiful January Sunday, singing hymns as they went, they climbed Hanaokayama, a hill to the southwest of Kumamoto. Here they solemnly made a covenant that they would labour to enlighten the darkness of their country by preaching the gospel even if it meant sacrificing their own lives.

The boys' parents were horrified. One mother told her son that if he did not abandon Christianity she would commit suicide to wipe out the stain he had cast upon his ancestors. Another parent informed his son more directly that if the boy did not give up the faith he would kill him immediately.[6] Such a reaction might seem extreme and many of the poor boys were indeed cruelly persecuted, but the parents deserve some sympathy. They had been brought up to believe that Christianity was an evil, foreign sect. Seeing their sons caught up in such a fever of belief in this "wicked" religion must have produced fears similar to those experienced by a late twentieth-century parent whose child becomes ensnared by a bizarre cult religion.

Christianity in Kumamoto did not fare as well as in some other parts of Japan in the early 1880s. There was, however, a liberal faction in the town who, in the name of progress, while not professing the faith themselves, fought to silence intolerant opposition. At any rate John Brandram and his sister were able to take up permanent residence in 1887, and in the same year a church and a school were built.[7] Despite these encouragements, the task facing the small band of missionaries living in Kumamoto in 1891 was, by any standards, a daunting one.

After the long months of preparation to become missionaries, the lengthy sea voyage, and the temporary sojourn in Osaka, Hannah and Grace must have felt satisfaction at finally being lodged in their own house and at last ready to embark on the great task of bringing Christ to the Japanese people. But their eagerness to get on with the job was inhibited by the formidable language barrier, and for the first year the bulk of their time was taken up with the study of Japanese. In common with so many other missionaries working in Japan, their sense of frustration at the constraints imposed on their work by the sheer difficulty of the language comes across clearly in their letters sent back to CMS headquarters in London.

But because so many Japanese wanted to learn English and because the two foreign single ladies were themselves objects of considerable fascination, both Hannah and Grace were able to start teaching almost immediately. Hannah had an English class for young men three afternoons a week and a fourth class on Sunday, when one of her more earnest students would translate the lesson into Japanese. A member of their small church, he diligently came to No. 2 Choanji-cho on Saturday evenings to prepare the week's lesson with Hannah. The lesson had to be fully written out because, as Hannah wryly pointed out in a letter to the CMS, her Japanese and his English were about on a par, and if she were to become at all discursive, her young translator would have come to a grinding halt.[8]

The school from which these young men came was the Government College or Fifth Higher School, which was recognised as one of the best in the country. Even before Japan began to modernise, there was a relatively high level of literacy in the country, and in 1872 an ambitious plan to introduce a comprehensive system of education for everyone was announced. According to the plan, there were to be eight educational districts, each with its own university, thirty-two middle schools, and 6,720 primary schools.[9]

A number of teachers at the Kumamoto Fifth Higher School from the late nineteenth century are remembered even today. One was Natsume Soseki, the famous writer whose portrait appears on the current thousand-yen note. Another was Lafacadio Hearn, who taught English at the school between 1891 and 1894 and wrote a great deal about the experience. The students were, by today's standards, already mature, their ages ranging from an average of eighteen in the lowest class to twenty-five in the highest. The objective of the school was to prepare the young men for the Imperial University, for which they needed to pass immensely difficult examinations, including ones in Chinese, English, and either French or German. When the men were not studying, they spent much of their time dressed in military uniforms performing drill. Hearn described the students as being tough and disciplined in the samurai tradition. The Western writer approved of Japanese traditions as much as he disapproved of Christian missionaries. On the latter he made his views very plain:

Probably missionaries must be tolerated for some time longer, in spite of their interference in matters altogether outside of their profession; but they will accomplish no moral good, and in the interim they will be used by those whom they desire to use.[10]

Hearn specifically distrusted single lady missionaries, as shown in this excerpt from one of his letters:

The missionaries are furthermore wrong in sending women to the old-fashioned districts. The people do not understand the maiden-missionary, and if she receives a single foreign visitor not of her own sex, the most extraordinary stories are set in circulation. Of course, the people are not malicious in the matter; but they find such a life contrary to all their own social experience, and they judge it falsely in consequence.

For myself I could sympathize with the individual but never with the missionary-cause. Unconsciously, every honest being in the mission-army is a destroyer—and a destroyer only; for nothing can replace what they break down. Unconsciously, too, the missionaries everywhere represent the edge . . . of Occidental aggression. We are face to face here with the spectacle of a powerful and selfish civilization demoralizing and crushing a weaker and, in many ways, a nobler one . . . and the spectacle is not pretty.[11]

Hearn's strong views on missionaries made it unlikely that he and Hannah would have seen much of each other, although Hearn's students almost certainly were among those who sought extra English tuition from Hannah. Of course, many of these young men came to Hannah and Grace's little house in Choanji-cho more to learn English than to discover Christ. This was a problem many missionaries faced and one which partly explains why so many Japanese "Christians" fell away after they had completed their studies. A number of students, however, were genuinely impressed by what they heard of Christianity, and Hannah was soon able to claim some successes. Grace, meanwhile, held an English class for young women three afternoons a week and a Bible class for them on Sundays. For some reason, it is not a surprise to discover that Hannah taught the young men and Grace the ladies.

Busy though the two women were with studying and teaching, soon after their arrival in Kumamoto they found time to visit the Honmyoji temple, an experience that was to shape the rest of Hannah's life. The temple lies on the northern outskirts of the city, an easy jinrikisha's ride from where Hannah and Grace were living. Honmyoji is a splendid temple but it was neither its fine setting nor the striking architecture that caught Hannah's eye on that first occasion—it was leprosy.

10

Leprosy

Leprosy, especially with its Biblical connotations, would have been famil-
iar enough to Hannah, but it is unlikely that before her first visit to the
Honmyoji temple she had ever actually seen anyone with the disease.
The experience was a dramatic one, as is clear from the impassioned
account she gave in her first annual report written to the CMS on 1
December 1891:

> About three-quarters of an hour's walk from the city is the tomb of
> the man who built the castle here some centuries ago. It is ap-
> proached by means of a long, rudely-paved street with an avenue of
> cherry-trees. All the way along on either side are temples and
> shrines, and the house of the priests who preside therein; then
> comes a flight of some two hundred steps or so, and at the top is the
> sacred tomb of Mr. Kato: in front of it is a temple. In the temple, and
> before the shrine, incense and candles are perpetually burning, and
> in the temple and before the shrine are <u>lepers</u> in every degree of
> loathsomeness, beseeching the spirit in the tomb for cleansing.
> Those who can walk go to the incense urn, take out some ashes, and
> rub them on themselves, or take a little holy water and pour it over
> them. On one side is a shelter where a big drum is beaten loudly and
> quickly, and the poor "vain repetitions" to the spirit in the tomb
> keep time with the drum-beats. Last time I went a boy about

sixteen, looking very ghastly, was sitting in front of the drum, his eyes shut, and turning his head sharply from side to side at each beat of the drum, and repeating his prayer the while—probably a penance enjoined by the priests. The noise alone was overwhelming. These lepers spend their all on doctors before going there. Destitute, homeless, in unutterable misery, sleeping under bridges or by the road-side, they drag out the remainder of their wretched lives. They want a Father Damien [the famous Catholic priest who worked with lepers in Hawaii and eventually himself succumbed to the disease]. Is there not one among the CMS recruits? I have no medical experience, but I could see that advice was carried out and take a little comfort to them.

Hannah had found her life's work. Here was a group of people forced to beg for their very existence. They had been abandoned and rejected by their own society, and their only hope lay in supplication to "heathen" gods. They were a group, moreover, that had been singled out by Christ Himself as especially worthy of salvation. In her subsequent writings, Hannah makes it clear that from her first encounter with the lepers she felt this was the work that God intended for her and was the reason He had brought her to Japan.

There were a number of reasons why the unfortunate lepers gathered at Honmyoji. The temple was dedicated to the great Kato Kiyomasa, the same man who had built Kumamoto Castle, the general who had fought with Hideyoshi against Korea in the sixteenth century, and a devoted adherent of the Nichiren sect of Buddhism. Kiyomasa himself was said to have suffered from leprosy, and while this story was almost certainly untrue, it made his tomb a magnet for lepers, some of whom came from great distances seeking a cure at the site where his ashes lay. Indeed, Kato Kiyomasa was the protector of all the temples of Hokke—the Buddhist sect founded by Nichiren—and lepers were generally to be found in their precincts.

Nichiren, born in 1222, was apparently a meditative and dreamy child, but this tranquility of temperament was not to last. The monk's adult life was stormy and controversial. The sect he founded was largely a reaction to the popular Shin and Jodo sects and became one of the largest, most influential, and—some would say—most bigoted in Japan. Nichiren produced many brilliant intellects but also bred intolerance and arrogance, vigorously asserting all other forms of Buddhism to be wrong and fiercely rejecting Christianity.

> No other sect is so fond of controversy. The bonzes [priests] of none other can excel those of the Nichiren sect in proselytising zeal, in the bitterness of their theological arguments, in the venom of their reviling, or the force with which they hurl their epithets at those who differ in opinion or practice from them.[1]

Pantheism was a hallmark of Nichiren's beliefs. The sect also exhibited a fiery patriotism and deep reverence for the Buddhist scriptures, particularly the Hokkekyo (hence an alternative name of the sect, Hokke), which was itself worshipped. In *Out of the East* Lafcadio Hearn wrote that the sacred invocation of *namu-myo-ho-renge-kyo* [Hail O Sutra of the Lotus of the Wonderful Law] echoed like "the roar of surf" around the temple of Honmyoji.

Along with other Buddhist sects, the Nichiren taught that the sins committed by an individual in one existence would be punished in subsequent lives, and leprosy was regarded as a heavy mark of retribution for previous misdeeds. But the sect also preached that remission of sins could be won by benevolence. Consequently, followers of Nichiren willingly gave alms to the miserable human beings they found crowding the steps of the Honmyoji temple. Their fearful appearance was an only too graphic reminder of the fate that awaited the sinful and uncharitable. Honmyoji, therefore, was a mecca for the destitute, and no group of people was more destitute than the lepers.

After her first confrontation with leprosy at Honmyoji, probably sometime in the spring of 1891, Hannah devoted most of her life to working for its victims. Unfortunately she did not live to see the major breakthrough in the treatment of the disease, which occurred, nine years after her death, with the introduction of sulfone drugs in 1941. Many of the more mysterious aspects of leprosy that eluded Hannah's scientific and medical contemporaries have been clarified, but there remain, even in the late twentieth century, a number of unanswered questions which continue to puzzle the experts.

What exactly is the nature of this affliction which has wrought such havoc among human beings and which Hannah Riddell, along with countless others, spent her life confronting? It is worth taking a closer look at the disease which, for many reasons both physiological and sociological, is markedly different from any other.

In the *Leprosy Review* in 1977 N. H. Antia wrote that "leprosy is a disease which affects the body of the patient and the mind of the public," a statement which rings true whenever or wherever the disease has appeared. In the West leprosy has not been a major problem since the late Middle Ages, and yet the very word leper is one of the most vivid in the English language, instantly conjuring up visions of hideous deformity, ostracism, and profound human misery.

Leprosy is an infectious disease spread, mostly it seems, by coughing and sneezing, although the debate over exactly how it is contracted continues today. Only a small percentage of the population at large is susceptible to leprosy but it flourishes in conditions of poverty and overcrowding. The villain of the piece is a bacillus called *Mycobacterium leprae*. This microscopic, rod-shaped organism destroys the victim's peripheral nerves and affects the skin and sometimes the eye, respiratory tract, testes, muscles, and bones. The bacillus was initially isolated in 1874 by a Norwegian doctor, G. Armauer Hansen, and was the very first bacterium to be identified as causing disease in man.

Disappointment followed this epoch-making discovery because, despite many attempts, scientists were unable to infect either themselves or any animal with the bacterium, nor were they successful in efforts to culture it in an artificial medium in a laboratory. This failure made studying the organism very difficult and was all the more baffling since other bacteria (including those which cause tuberculosis, similar to *Mycobacterium leprae*) were discovered not long afterwards and presented no such problems. Not until 1960 did scientists finally achieve a limited success when leprosy was transmitted to the foot-pads of mice.

Another reason why leprosy has been so hard to investigate and bring under control is the extraordinarily slow rate at which it develops. Most bacteria that attack man reproduce themselves in a matter of minutes, whereas the leprosy bacillus takes nearly two weeks. This means that the incubation period and development of the disease are unusually long, making leprosy especially difficult to track. Moreover, like all clever parasites that wreak such terrible damage, these bacteria stop short of killing their hosts. Before modern drugs, the victims of leprosy were condemned to live out their lives, sometimes for many decades, crippled by slowly deteriorating and terrible deformities, despised and feared by the world at large. It is little wonder, therefore, that leprosy has always induced such dread and has borne a stigma carried by no other disease.

Christians have long been in the forefront of caring for leprosy sufferers, perhaps inspired by Christ's command to his disciples to "cleanse the lepers" [Matthew 10: 8] and perhaps because the disease is given such a high profile in the Bible as a symbol of the kind of suffering and neglect true Christians should try to alleviate. Ironically (although Hannah would not have known this) the disease mentioned in the Bible is not the leprosy that is caused by Hansen's bacterium. Scholarly analysis suggests that the biblical references refer to a whole host of conditions which, for ritualistic reasons, rendered an individual "unclean," a judgement generally made by the temple priest and which had little to do with clinical diagnosis.[2]

The earliest physical evidence of true leprosy comes from Egypt in the shape of four leprous skulls buried in the second century B.C. Records written four centuries earlier in India accurately describe the disease, and leprosy probably originated either in India or Africa. From India this unwelcome export arrived in China, where, in 190 B.C., in a surprisingly modern analysis, environmental factors such as overcrowding and unhygienic conditions were listed as among the causes of leprosy. The disease continued its eastward progress to Japan and was probably carried westward by the soldiers of Alexander the Great returning from his Indian campaign.

Over the centuries leprosy became prevalent in numerous societies and cultures but most of them, however diverse, had one reaction in common—the association of leprosy with sin. This assumption that leprosy was a punishment inflicted by the gods coupled with the fear of contagion did little to improve the leper's lot. In parts of China victims were burned alive if rich or buried alive if poor. In Nigeria some victims even requested live burial in order to protect others. In Europe too there were countless instances of lepers being burned, buried, and starved to death, and it is hard to imagine a more chilling experience than being the subject of a "leper's mass." The priest intoned over the victim's hooded and shrouded figure words that were in effect banishment from the human race, forbidding him "to enter church, market-places, the mill, the bakehouse, the assembly of the people . . . I forbid thee to go abroad without thy leper uniform."[3]

But it would be wrong to infer that no attempts were made in earlier times to relieve the suffering caused by leprosy. The medieval orders of chivalry were deeply involved in succouring such social outcasts, notably the Order of St. Lazarus of Jerusalem, founded in 1050, whose early masters were themselves lepers.[4] Warriors returning from the Crusades gave both impetus to the spread of leprosy and a public-relations headache to the ecclesiastical authorities. How was it possible that these Christian soldiers who had fought so bravely for their faith should return home scarred by this most terrible of divine punishments? The official answer to the paradox was that, as a reward for their endeavours, they were being privileged to share the Lord's suffering. It is difficult to imagine this argument gave much comfort to the poor soldiers, but the end of the eleventh century did witness some improvement in the treatment of lepers with the building of a number of hospices and alms-houses especially for them.

In Japan the individual first associated with the care of lepers was Empress Komyo, who built a hospice for lepers in Nara in the eighth century. Tradition claims the Empress was beautiful but not afraid to go to the hospital and wash and dress the sores of its patients. In the sixteenth and seventeenth centuries various attempts were made by Catholics specifically to help lepers, and hospitals were founded in Nagasaki, Osaka, and other places. A number of lepers became converts, and some even suffered execution for their faith.

In Europe leprosy peaked in the thirteenth and fourteenth centuries and then gradually died out. Exactly why it disappeared at that time is not known but the Black Death may have killed off the great majority of lepers, already weakened by disease. The last indigenous leper in Britain died as long ago as 1798[5] but in Japan it was sadly a different story. Some estimates put the number of leprosy victims in Japan towards the end of the last century as high as 150,000. The first official nationwide survey in 1900 claimed there were 30,359. Whatever the true figure, leprosy was unquestionably a serious problem in Meiji Japan and there was little or no provision to deal with it.

The Confucian ethic, so deeply ingrained in the Japanese psyche, resulted in most problems concerned with sickness and old age being taken care of by close relatives. Such affairs were considered the responsibility of the individuals involved, and the state played little or no part. Leprosy, however, produced a different set of rules. Because of the terrible shame attached to the disease, those who caught it were often thrown out of their homes, forced to live in beggarly isolation, or went into voluntary exile rather than disgrace their families and destroy their lives. As the observant Mary Fraser pointed out in A *Diplomatist's Wife in Japan*, "Such cruelty is really foreign to the national character; nowhere is there more help and kindness shown in the family and tribe than in Japan." Most hospitals refused to accept lepers, though Mary wrote that she had visited one hospital where she saw leprosy, typhoid, and diphtheria patients all in the same ward.

No doubt there were Buddhist temples that showed kindness or gave shelter to vagrant lepers but apart from Empress Komyo's contribution in the eighth century, the first recorded formal leprosy refuge in Japan run by Japanese was the Kaiten Hospital, which was opened in Gifu in 1874 by a Buddhist priest. It is, however, a handful of Christians who take the greatest credit for focussing on the plight of Japanese lepers in the late nineteenth century and who were responsible for opening most of the early hospitals to assist them. These Christian missionaries, both Protestant and Catholic, may have been drawn to leprosy because of its biblical connotations and because they saw an opportunity to evangelise, but there is little reason to doubt that their primary motive was simply one of philanthropy.

Hannah Riddell was not the first foreigner in the field. In 1889 a French Catholic missionary, Father Germain-Leger Testevuide, bought a house to care for about six patients in the small village of Gotemba at the foot of Mount Fuji. The story goes that, by accident, Father Testevuide discovered a woman in the advanced stages of leprosy dying slowly and alone in a deserted hut. Having tried unsuccessfully to admit her into a hospital, the priest decided to care for the woman himself. Seared by this experience, he won the sanction of his bishop to found a refuge for leprosy sufferers and there gave them a course of treatment recommended by Dr. Masafumi Goto, at that time the only Japanese doctor seriously interested in leprosy. Predictably the villagers did not much like the idea of an expanding leper colony in their midst, and the good father was soon asked, in no uncertain terms, to move on. With his limited funds, Father Testevuide bought a few acres on which he was able to build his hospital and grow some food and was soon able to care for about eighty patients. This noble venture survived the Second World War and was still in existence in 1995.

Kate Youngman, an American, was like Testevuide one of the first foreigners to focus on the leprosy problem. Sent to Japan in 1873 by the Presbyterians to start a school for Japanese girls, she was soon diverted into leprosy relief work. She bought land in the Meguro section of Tokyo to build a small leprosarium in 1894, the year before Hannah Riddell opened her hospital a thousand miles away in Kumamoto.

11

Hannah

There is reason for thankfulness in the knowledge that our missionary ranks are now so fully constituted of men and women of culture
and good breeding, who understand how to meet courtesy by courtesy and to sympathize with and reciprocate gentleness of demeanour.[1]

The author of the above paragraph had obviously not met Hannah
Riddell. Hannah was different. She did not comfortably fit the mould of
the gentle, lady-like missionary so beloved of the CMS, and her colleagues were soon made painfully aware of this fact. Female missionaries
had not been long in the field, and although many were to show extraordinary courage and initiative in the face of great trials, there was no
question that abroad, as at home, they were under the command of men.

Hannah knew the rules of Victorian society as well as any woman, but
with her self-confessed love of "organising" and her natural authority, she
clearly chafed under male domination. There is no evidence to suggest
she actively supported the suffragettes but throughout her life she be-
haved with a will and determination that by the standards of the time
were distinctly unfeminine. She liked to identify a problem and then deal
with it, and if misguided people chose to place obstacles in her way, she
was adept, some might even say Machiavellian, in circumnavigating
them.

Once Hannah had seen the nature of the problem at Honmyoji, she resolved, with Grace's support, to do something about it, and within a matter of months of arriving in Kumamoto launched herself into action. She quickly concluded that the aim should be the establishment of a hospital specifically built to meet the needs of leprosy patients. Such a major and worthy project was an exciting challenge and one that Hannah, with her particular abilities, immediately embarked on with conviction and persistence.

Although her personal relationships, particularly with her own countrymen, were often fraught with tension and difficulty, Hannah undoubtedly had a natural flair for public relations. She instinctively knew how best to attract attention to her cause, and in the interests of making a point more effectively or dramatically, she was not, on occasion, afraid to sacrifice accuracy.

Intriguingly this is the case with the much publicised account of her very first visit to Honmyoji, a tale that Hannah was to relate countless times over the next forty years on her fund-raising campaigns both in lectures and published articles. "Honmyoji—first saw lepers" is clearly inscribed in her own hand on the day of 3 April in her *Daily Light* prayerbook. She would tell of how she had gone to the temple to see the cherry blossom several years after her arrival in Japan the day of a great festival. But the fact is she must have seen the lepers not two years but almost immediately after she arrived in Kumamoto because both she and Grace wrote about the experience in their first official letters to the CMS, dated 1 December and 9 December 1891 respectively. Equally, it could not have been 3 April 1891 because on that day she was in Osaka attending the CMS conference.

It is, of course, possible that she just forgot the details but more likely Hannah consciously (or unconsciously) compressed several visits made to Honmyoji over a period of time, extracted the most striking elements of each occasion, and fashioned them into one good story. She would have considered such methods entirely justified if they achieved her objective of stirring the public conscience and winning support for the relief of the lepers. In this objective, Hannah was soon at odds with a number of her fellow missionaries.

John Brandram, the sensitive and hard-pressed priest already some seven years in the field when Hannah arrived, was tormented by the knowledge of the vast numbers of unconverted souls in his area. He liked to climb Hanaokayama, the hill behind the Anglican church (where twenty years earlier the ardent young Japanese boys had sworn their pledge to Christ) from where there was a fine view over the entire city of Kumamoto. But, as May Freeth, another Kyushu missionary, noted in a letter written in 1897, it was a view that often overwhelmed him, as it was such a vivid reminder of his enormous responsibilities.

Brandram's recent marriage to Mary Smith, the daughter of a missionary and herself one of the first female workers sent to Japan, must have improved life for him, but for the most part Brandram's time in Kumamoto had not been easy. In 1890 not only were the Buddhists becoming more active but, even worse, the despised Unitarian Colonel Olcott had been holding meetings in the city. Politics were absorbing the country in an unprecedented manner, especially in Kumamoto Province, where the conservative and anti-foreign party chose to focus on the Christians as "the enemy." The feelings of the Kyushu Christians were summed up by Archibald Hutchinson, the veteran CMS missionary in Fukuoka, who wrote, "Alas! For these times of strong political passion, they take men's minds off from the one thing needful."[2]

Indeed, the number of baptisms—the missionaries' most important yardstick in judging their success or failure—was generally down, the figure for the whole of Japan in 1890 being 2,135.[3] Not only were there fewer baptisms but there was also a worrying number of defections, about six hundred a year across the country.[4] To make matters worse for John Brandram, he suffered a personal blow when his sister, who had lived and worked with him in Japan for a number of years but had been forced to return home because of poor health, died in 1892.

Brandram welcomed the idea of lady workers in Japan with the caveat that they should not be "from a humble social position" but his more pressing concern was to have a greater number of trained Japanese workers rather than fresh missionaries from England. As for Hannah's plans for a leprosy hospital, he was not enthusiastic. He felt that as long as there were two and a half million "heathen" in his district, the primary task must be one of evangelisation. With this sentiment he was reflecting not only official CMS policy but also the views of many of his fellow missionaries who considered that now that so many Japanese had been trained by Western (mainly German) doctors, there was much less need for medical missionary work and they should all be concentrating their efforts on gathering lost Japanese sheep into the Christian fold.

At the time Hannah arrived in Kumamoto at the beginning of 1891, morale was at a particularly low ebb, a fact even acknowledged by the normally optimistic official CMS history, which attributed this gloomy state of affairs to a "lack of unity among the converts." Brandram, therefore, had good reason to feel professionally depressed, and it must have been more than a little irksome to come up against the full force of Hannah's fresh ideas and enthusiasm. He had been labouring long years against difficult odds, working exhausting hours and often experiencing physical discomfort and loneliness. Now, within weeks of arriving at her new post, this large, energetic, but totally inexperienced woman was purposefully canvassing support for a radical project, moreover, one with which Brandram had only lukewarm sympathy.

Before many months had passed, Hannah and Grace had the opportunity to try out their ideas on some visiting VIPs. The Bishop of Exeter and his family arrived in Kumamoto by train late on the night of 9 November 1891. Trains were still something of a novelty in Kumamoto, the railway company having only just been inaugurated the previous July on the same day as the electric-light company. Electricity was at first little used except by the garrison but the railway was another matter, as it put Kumamoto in closer touch with the rest of Japan, making Osaka, for instance, only two days away. From the missionaries' point of view the coming of the railway meant they could visit their out-stations more easily and penetrate yet further into rural Japan.

The bishop's party consisted of his second wife, Mrs. Bickersteth, his daughter, Mary, and his son, the energetic and dynamic Anglican bishop in Japan, Edward Bickersteth. Such distinguished visitors must have caused something of a stir in the small expatriate community in Kumamoto and no doubt considerable effort went into the planning of their stay. The Bishop of Exeter together with his wife and son stayed with the Brandrams, while Mary was lodged with Hannah and Grace.

12

Visitors

Edward Bickersteth, was not only a rising star but also a member of one of the most distinguished ecclesiastical families in England. His father was a famous bishop, and his grandfather had been secretary to the CMS; indeed, most members of his family were connected in one way or another with the church. A successful schoolboy, Edward Bickersteth went on to have a brilliant career at Cambridge, before, under the auspices of The Society of the Propagation of the Gospel, going to India, where he founded the Cambridge University Mission. After about five years he was forced to return to England for health reasons but, as a result of Bishop Poole's premature death, he found himself in 1886, at the young age of thirty-five, bound for Japan as the newly appointed Anglican bishop.

In Japan he discovered the church in some disarray, lacking both coherence and unity. The SPG and CMS often appeared more like rivals than colleagues, while communication with the American church, also active in the field, was poor. A man of great vigour, Bickersteth constantly travelled from one end of the country to the other, stirring the missionaries to even greater efforts. But his biggest contribution to Christian life in Japan was the key role he played in moulding the different Anglican churches into one native church, the Nippon Seikokai, founded in 1886, shortly after his arrival.

Meanwhile, Bickersteth's sister, Mary, was working in London for the St. Paul's Guild, an organisation that raised money for missionary work in

Japan. She wrote a book about her family's expedition to Japan, *Japan as We Saw It*, and, as the following passages illustrate, was a humorous and intelligent observer of the scene:

> At the station we found a police inspector in charge, who, after helping us to find our luggage, ushered us into the waiting-room. He was a very courteous man, evidently a Samurai, one of the warrior class, many of whom lost nearly everything at the Revolution, and were thankful to enter the ranks of the army or police force. But we were much amused, and very grateful, when, soon after he had settled us in the waiting-room, he reappeared, accompanied by a maid who carried a dainty tray of tea and cakes, which he offered us with many bows, after delicately tasting the tea to make sure that it was good. We felt that we were in Japan indeed, for an English police inspector might conceivably have managed the tea, but never the bows.

The following evening, having called on the officer in charge in the castle where they were served coffee (still a rarity and a luxury in Japan), the Bickersteth party, the Brandrams, Hannah, and Grace all went down to the mission church, where Mary's father preached to a "large and attentive congregation of converts."[1] Mary reports how, at first, the mission had made rapid progress and the people had built their church largely through their own exertions. Women had given the proceeds of their knitting, a farmer a share of the profits of his poultry yard, and a hotel keeper a percentage of his till. She alludes to recent difficulties, pointing out that "the work of a foreign Mission among such a people is one of peculiar delicacy, and we were scarcely surprised to hear that the first fervour of the people of Kumamoto had been followed by an outbreak of independence as regards Church matters, which had resulted in a serious check to the growth of the congregation. But the check promises to be a passing one, and all hope that, with wise management, the marked Japanese characteristic of a due respect for law and order will prevail at Kumamoto as in other parts of Japan."[2]

After the service, the missionaries repaired to the schoolroom, where they enjoyed cakes, sweets, and persimmons:

> We all sat on the floor, as usual, and at every polite remark the heads

of the audience bent forward, and reminded me vividly of the effect produced by the wind as it passes over a field of wheat. We knew it was strict Japanese etiquette to take away any food not consumed at the time, and a piece of paper was provided for the purpose. But our portions that night were very large and sticky, and my hostess, Miss Riddell, thought that her cook might safely bring home what we had left in one parcel. But she had evidently reckoned without our hosts in the matter. Just as I had settled myself in my jinrikisha, a delightfully polite Japanese came, with many bows, and put my rejected sweets in my lap. They were of all sizes and shapes, and I had an exciting ride home trying to prevent one sticky possession after another from making its escape into the road.[3]

The men went on a manly expedition to Mount Aso, where the crater duly impressed them with its continuous roar as it belched out sulphur, smoke, and steam. The trip to the volcano was considered too difficult for the ladies, who went sightseeing in Kumamoto. Mary witnessed one of Hannah's classes and was much impressed by the determination of the young men to learn English. She was also amused to learn of one pupil who had requested to board with Hannah and Grace but had promised to "arrange for the keeping of his body."[4]

On 12 November Hannah and Grace took their guest to Honmyoji. Mary describes how they walked through a street of shops, in which small shrines with figures of Kiyomasa and Buddhist rosaries could be bought. The boy Hannah had noticed on previous visits to the temple was still there, maniacally shaking his head from side to side as he prayed. Behind the image of Kiyomasa, a woman rocked backwards and forwards, and in the courtyard "a man ran up and down muttering his prayers, apparently afraid of breaking some vow if he stopped for a moment."[5]

The three English ladies, clad in their long Victorian dresses and doubtless wearing hats, must have made an incongruous group against the backdrop of Honmyoji's splendid flight of stone steps with its tragic occupants. However different the three women may have been in character they were certainly united in their longing "for the days when powerful Christian influence in the land will render such a temple an impossibility."[6] But until Hannah and Grace's plans came to fruition, they could only "trust that the groanings of those poor lepers did reach to heaven, though the true God was so utterly unknown to them."[7]

13

Launching the
Hospital

The CMS required every missionary to make an annual written report, and a couple of weeks after the Bickersteth visit, Grace and Hannah each submitted a formal account of their first year as missionaries. Half of Hannah's was taken up with an impassioned description of the lepers at Honmyoji, and both women concluded their letters by pleading for a CMS initiative to alleviate the situation.

The response of the CMS secretary, Crispian Fenn, written to Grace the following March was bureaucratic. He questioned how such an operation would be financed and staffed but his main concern was with the wisdom of targeting lepers. Fenn's underlying point is clear: should valuable resources be spent on a segment of the community who could do so little to contribute to the building up of the Christian church in Japan?

This view was entirely consistent with CMS thinking on its role in Japan. The society was in the business of winning souls—lots of them. Obviously a proposal as worthy as a leprosy hospital could not be ignored, but it was nevertheless a side line, one that should not be allowed to interfere with the main thrust of missionary work.

Undeterred by any lack of enthusiasm from headquarters, Hannah and Grace continued to plot and to plan how best they might further their hospital scheme. Sometime during the spring of 1892 they succeeded in arousing the interest of an influential Japanese named Dr. Eijiro Haga, the principal garrison doctor of the Sixth Division of the imperial army, stationed at Kumamoto Castle. Haga was a rising star of the medical establishment and a man of spirit and initiative. In 1897, when he left Kumamoto, he represented Japan at several Red Cross conferences in Europe, afterwards choosing to return to his own country on horseback across Siberia. When Haga saw one of Wilhelm K. Roentgen's early X-ray machines in a German military hospital, he was so impressed that he bought one out of his own pocket and had it sent to the Army Medical College in Tokyo.

Haga and Hannah were made for each other, and in May, Hannah wrote to Crispian Fenn with scarcely concealed excitement about Haga's reaction to her plans for the hospital. She and Grace had asked two Japanese members of the church committee to help gather information about leprosy and plan their strategy. These two men were Professor Masujiro Honda and Hisashi Kanazawa. Without their consistent and loyal support over many years Hannah would never have been able to achieve all that she did.

Like Lafcadio Hearn, Honda was an English teacher at the Fifth Higher School and already a Christian by the time he met Hannah in 1891. Kanazawa had been stationed in Kumamoto with the army since 1887 and in his spare time had been taking English lessons, first with John Brandram and then with Hannah. Honda and Kanazawa approached Haga, who judged the hospital a splendid idea, saying that only Christians would have thought of such a thing. He also said that if the two ladies were to succeed in the project he would help them all he could.

Unfortunately Haga's understanding of leprosy seems to have been as muddled as most other people's at the time, although he was a doctor and despite the fact that Hansen's breakthrough had occurred nearly twenty years earlier. Haga believed Japanese leprosy to be non-infectious because it was so "old." He described it as hereditary but said that it often skipped generations, and he thought that in Kumamoto there was not one family wholly free from it. According to Hannah, he held that those in whom the disease lay dormant were especially beautiful. He also claimed, alas wrongly, that up to seventy percent of Japanese lepers could be cured if they had treatment soon enough after the onset of the disease.

Despite Haga's misconceptions, his approval of the scheme was clearly a great boost to Hannah, who wrote in a letter to Crispian Fenn "that he, a heathen, should be so strongly in our favour and ready to help is delightful beyond words." She added, "I am anxious not to say much about it among the Japanese because the Romanists are very active here and would probably act on <u>our</u> idea without delay if they heard of it."

She continued her letter with a discussion of the problem of finding a suitable doctor for the hospital, agreeing with Fenn that "a zealous Christian Japanese doctor" would be the best. She modestly confessed that those of her friends who already knew of her plans had suggested that she herself should be the doctor. However, she quickly followed this remark by professing "I think myself a man is better but certainly, if it were thought that it would help matters on, I would gladly go through any course of training likely to make me an efficient helper. At present I have had some little experience in home-nursing only, and my friends say a natural aptitude for it."

The timing of this letter to Fenn is important because it was written when Brandram was away from Kumamoto. Hannah, bursting with enthusiasm for her project, had clearly failed to convince her immediate superior of its merits. By writing to Fenn while Brandram was absent she was attempting to outmanoeuvre him, a tactic she was often to employ and in doing so infuriate her opponents. Tellingly she wrote, "You may perhaps know that Mr. Brandram left Kumamoto in April, but hopes to return for a visiting tour to the out-stations with Mr. Evington early in June. At that time I hope to ask him, or rather tell him, of our having written to you and of your reply. Mr. Brandram will probably reach England in August and then perhaps, if you think it desirable, you can talk to him about it. I have twice essayed the subject, preparatory to mentioning our own wishes, but was met with such a flat 'I know nothing at all about them' that I never got further than expressing my compassion for their state, wishing it could be relieved." She follows this with a sentence that is surely a *cri de coeur*: "Old missionaries seem to have a chronic fear of new missionaries starting new ideas."

There may have been the odd truce over the next seven and a half years, but the battle lines between Hannah and John Brandram had been unmistakably drawn and were eventually to result in tragedy. But for the time being, they were temporarily relieved of each other's company because in the summer of 1892 the Brandrams sailed for England and a well-earned furlough, leaving Hannah and Grace without a resident clerical missionary for many months.

The two ladies made the most of Brandram's absence to drum up further support for the hospital. In April, Bishop Bickersteth was back in Kumamoto for just one night and appears to have been convinced by their arguments. Unlike Fenn, he could see the point of setting a Christian example which would surely not go unnoticed in a town where there was considerable anti-Christian sentiment. But it is striking that in weighing up the pros and cons of the proposed hospital, no one in authority at the CMS appears to have been much concerned with alleviating the actual suffering of the lepers. In their urgent desire to Christianise Japan CMS officials had become blinkered, failing to see that Hannah, with her genuine longing to do something for a wretched group of human beings, was preaching the most powerful Christian message of all.

Quick to exploit the bishop's interest, Hannah sent a present of Kumamoto crafts to Fenn and at the same time pressed him to commit CMS funds to the hospital. He replied that though he was glad to hear of the bishop's interest in the proposed leper hospital, the CMS could do nothing until it heard from the annual conference, the newly appointed finance committee, or at least the archdeacon. Once again Hannah was employing her usual tactics of ignoring established channels and going straight to the top, hoping thereby to present any dissenting colleagues with a *fait accompli*.

Both Hannah and Grace were also busy with more conventional missionary duties. Hannah's work with the young men was proving enjoyable and fruitful. About twelve students from the Fifth Higher School came to her for advanced English lessons. More surprising, she was able to draw around twenty boys for her Sunday Bible class, which was conducted in Japanese through an interpreter. Hannah was an articulate, intelligent woman who spoke with passion, and consequently her missionary efforts were rewarded.

She found that the biggest problem with her young students—and it was a difficulty shared by many missionaries in Japan—was to convince them of the concept of sin and of their need for salvation. The Japanese did not consider themselves sinners. Nor, indeed, did they experience guilt in the Christian sense and did not therefore want to be "saved." Hannah was also shocked to find that Japanese children were not taught to pray, even to their own gods. She came to the conclusion that religion in Japan was primarily regarded as a solace for those on a downward slope. Armed, however, with an unshakeable faith, a portable organ, and a magic lantern for showing slides, Hannah was confident that this could all be changed.

While Hannah concentrated on the men, Grace continued her work with the women. She gave German lessons and ran a Sunday Bible class which she admitted in a letter was "compared with Miss Riddell's for young men very small." Having found that there was little market among the women for English lessons, she sensibly started a dorcas meeting where one member of the group read aloud from Japanese translations of *Christie's Old Organ* or *Pilgrim's Progress,* while the others industriously sewed clothes for the children left destitute by the terrible earthquake of 28 October 1891, the worst for several decades in western Japan.

The epicentre of the earthquake was in Gifu but even in Osaka, about one hundred miles away, the tremors were strong enough to do severe damage. The Bickersteth party was staying at the time with Miss Tristram and, according to Mary's account, her father, the Bishop of Exeter, had a narrow escape when the walls of his room came crashing down. Many missionaries, among them the redoubtable Miss Tristram, hurried to the worst affected areas to help with the relief work. They were met by scenes of total devastation:

> Torn embankments, ripped up railroad tracks, great fissures in the earth, sunken bridges, deflected watercourses, villages knocked flat and smoking ruins.[1]

But amongst all this destruction Archdeacon Warren, who visited the area several days later, discovered a silver lining, which he recorded in his report on the earthquake: "The earthquake has opened a door for the exhibition of practical Christianity, the influence of which is already being felt. There may be and are secondary causes for such calamities, but they are not without our Father's hand and this national calamity now afflicting Japan may be among the means He is using to awaken Japan in general, and the affected districts in particular, to a sense of their need for a loving God . . . the earthquake may have far-reaching effects in winning many to discard their old faith."

If the Japanese found it difficult to reconcile "a loving God" with the horror and misery confronting them in the wake of a strong earthquake, they could nevertheless have hardly failed to be impressed by the Christians' eagerness to help and their readiness to undergo danger and hardship on their behalf. For the most part, Hannah and her fellow missionaries in Japan lived a life of safety, even luxury, but those who did experience the terrors of a powerful earthquake or erupting volcano were unlikely ever to forget the ordeal.

In March 1893 Hannah offered a paper to the annual missionary conference, formally putting forward her ideas for the establishment of a leper hospital at Kumamoto. The paper was a masterly piece of work and shows Hannah at her best and most formidable. She had done her homework well, and her case for the hospital is presented clearly and persuasively. She knew her audience and how to reach it. In her opening sally she told them that the only organised relief for the estimated 200,000 lepers in Japan was provided by Roman Catholics, a point that would not have been lost on the rows of Low Church Anglicans sitting before her.

Hannah then touched their hearts by telling them how leprosy sufferers were often referred to as *hinin*, a word meaning not merely outcast but actually not human. She told them of the villages around Kumamoto entirely populated with lepers and gave them a vivid description of the miseries to be witnessed at the Honmyoji temple. Having stirred the missionaries' emotions, she turned to practicalities. She acknowledged her debt to Professor Honda for having assembled most of the facts in her report and for spending his summer holiday visiting the leprosy refuge at Gotemba. Honda had also met Dr. Masafumi Goto and Dr. Erwin Baelz, a famous German doctor practising in Tokyo.

As a result of Professor Honda's researches, a committee composed of Hannah, Grace, and others had concluded the best way forward was to build a hospital and put a Japanese Christian doctor in charge. Hannah could not resist at this juncture suggesting the CMS fund a foreign lady superintendent because "in Hawaii [where Father Damien had set up a leprosarium] great good was accomplished by the sisters being in residence as it were. Quarrelling stopped and many objectionable practices ceased by the mere fact of their presence." It is not difficult to guess who Hannah envisaged filling the job. In the interim, however, the institution could be under the control of a visiting superintendent. Nurses and domestic staff would be recruited from the healthier patients and the laundress could be the wife of a patient, glad of the opportunity to remain with her husband.

One problem remained—how much was it all going to cost?

Hannah had done her sums and gave her listeners a careful breakdown of expenses. A builder had presented an estimate for a hospital which would house forty patients (twenty men and twenty women), as well as the resident doctor and lady superintendent. There would be a large multi-purpose room in which morning and evening services could be held, consulting, dispensing, and operating rooms, as well as bathhouses, mortuary, and servants' quarters. For all this they would need one thousand *tsubo* of land (about four-fifths of an acre). Hannah reckoned that six hundred pounds would buy a good piece of land, build, furnish, and pay the running expenses of a hospital for six months. How to raise the money was another question but she felt confident that they would receive aid from a group called the Mission to Lepers in India, who had already contributed so much help to the lepers in China.

Hannah had given her audience plenty to think about, and ideas and money were soon forthcoming. The following May she was able to write jubilantly to Fenn: "As you already know, the idea of a leper hospital at Kumamoto was very heartily approved of by the Conference." At the ladies' conference, it had been suggested that pamphlets advertising the new cause should be prepared for sending home in letters, and she enclosed one for Fenn to see. She was able to boast that the three most senior Anglican clerics in Japan—Bishop Bickersteth, Archdeacon Warren, and the Reverend Henry Evington—had already offered subscriptions. They had collected 192 yen from the missionaries and had been delighted to receive a donation of two hundred pounds from the Mission to Lepers in India. At this stage Evington seems to have been co-operating, at least to the extent that he had accompanied Hannah and Grace to inspect a plot of land that might be suitable for the hospital. Hannah had the wind in her sails and was soon busy organising a new committee with duly appointed secretary and treasurer.

In the same letter to Fenn, Hannah made a clear bid to become officially linked to the hospital:

> If the Home Committee grant the request of the Conference for a <u>worker</u> specially for the lepers, will you take into consideration the fact that when Miss Nott and I first wrote to you about the lepers <u>we both offered for the work</u>? We shall be very grateful to you if you will remember that. Naturally there is some reluctance in sparing those who can <u>speak a little</u>, from the sparse numbers of missionaries in

the field already. On the other hand the poor sick folk <u>absolutely need</u> some one who can make themselves understood in their own tongue, more than those who are well and strong and have patience to <u>find</u> out what is meant. Someone fresh from England would be <u>useless</u>, not knowing the language, the customs of the country nor the people and their ways, (a study in itself). The responsibility seems beyond a newcomer. I love my present work very much and I do not wish to change. <u>Nor do I wish to choose</u>, and yet I love the idea of helping the lepers and if my work cannot go on in the Church and with the lepers simultaneously, please remember that I, <u>that we</u>, offered for the lepers in abeyance to the needs of the Mission in December 1891.

I think the Conference perhaps lost sight of the fact that if any lady lives <u>with the lepers</u> it must be <u>two</u> ladies, not one. The isolation would be too severe a strain for me, added to the depressing nature of the work day by day.

It is obvious that Hannah had already decided that she and Grace, together possibly with Ada when she eventually arrived in Japan, should be employed by the CMS to work in the leper hospital and that it was just a matter of writing a few letters to the right people before this was accomplished. Hannah may have been used to getting her way but on this occasion she was to find that she was up against some stiff opposition.

14

Completion

If Hannah was still hopeful that financial backing would be forthcoming from the CMS she was to be disappointed. At the end of 1893 she received a letter from Fenn making it clear the society's general funds were not applicable to her proposals. He changed the subject as soon as he decently could, returning to a familiar theme: "It is consoling to know that in the mean time there is an abundance of work in which you can be engaged—direct evangelistic spiritual work. The door is still open in Japan for preaching and hearing the Gospel, though the obstacles for its reception . . . seem as great as ever."

Despite the lack of CMS money, Hannah was able to report in January 1894 that "our funds are steadily going up, but they have not reached the sum we had hoped to begin with; however, we have a very substantial prospect of being able to open it by September or October of the present year. There have been delays from without and within but the loving Hand which 'holds the key of all unknown' will unlock the door for us at the right moment."

Hannah's forecast for the completion of the hospital was optimistic. The delays from "within" are a clear reference to the want of support from the CMS and her Kyushu colleagues but the "delays from without" were equally frustrating. Various pieces of land had been considered as possible sites for the hospital but the committee finally decided to buy a plot of four thousand *tsubo* (about three acres) at the foot of Tatsuta Hill to the northeast of Kumamoto.

It was and still is a lovely spot. Close to the Fifth Higher School (now Kumamoto University), it was an area Lafcadio Hearn knew well and in the odd hour between classes he would often climb the ridge behind the site of the hospital. Above a slope of terraced fields was an ancient, disused village cemetery from where there was a fine view over the vast, green Higo Plain to the blue hills beyond and the ever-smoking volcano, Mount Aso. Contemplating the landscape was a stone Buddha, seated on a lotus leaf, his meditative gaze slanting down between his half-closed eyelids and, as Hearn wrote in *Out of the East,* "smiling the smile of one who has received an injury not to be resented."

Just to the north of the hospital was land owned by the Hosokawa family. The Hosokawas had remained loyal to Tokugawa Ieyasu during the decisive Battle of Sekigahara in 1600 and had been subsequently rewarded with a fiefdom in northern Kyushu. In 1632 the Hosokawas moved to Kumamoto, displacing the heirs of Kato Kiyomasa. From the castle, where they quickly established themselves, they ruled the surrounding province of Higo as feudal lords until the last Tokugawa shogun was removed and Emperor Meiji came to power in 1868.

Close to the hospital, at the foot of Tatsuta Hill, lay the burial ground of the Hosokawa family. The ancestors' spirits live among tall trees and bamboo groves filled with the sound of running water and birdsong. The illusion of eternity is strengthened by the tombstones themselves, standing in a solemn row, solid and steadfast. Hosokawa Tadaoki's tomb is here together with that of his wife, Gracia, famous in Japanese history as a devout Christian lady who is alleged to have willingly died rather than be captured by her husband's enemies.

The hospital was ideally situated, near but not too near the town and surrounded by the peace and beauty which Hannah considered essential for the patients' welfare. The transaction was not, however, without its problems. After the contract had been signed, the owner of the land demanded more money for the well and before finally handing the land over, cut down and sold all the trees. Despite these difficulties, in December 1894 Grace reported that building plans were in the hands of the carpenters and two months later, on 10 February, work finally began. Although the contract stated that the hospital would be ready by 25 May, work was not completed until October 1895. Furthermore, a well-educat-

1. Mrs. Riddell, Hannah's mother, also called Hannah, photographed in Swansea around 1880. Mrs. Riddell was co-principal of Russell House until her death in 1886.

2. Hannah's study in Russell House, Oystermouth. Hannah ran the school from 1877 until 1889, when she was declared bankrupt. This cosy room, with its well-stocked bookshelves, suggests more affluent times.

3. *Left:* Japan, the reality. Women refuel a ship by handing baskets of coal up ladders.

4. *Above:* Japan, the ideal. This postcard sums up the popular image of Japan held by many Europeans at the turn of the century.

5. A group of missionaries that includes Grace Nott on the far right, Hannah seated next to her, and the Reverend Albert Fuller and his wife standing.

6. Mount Aso, northeast of Kumamoto, belching out steam and sulphur in 1905.

7. A village in Gifu Prefecture destroyed by the 1891 earthquake.

8. Grace Nott in November 1890.   9. Hannah in early 1891.

10. A view of Kumamoto from the summit of Hanaokayama in the 1890s.

11. The Fifth Higher School, where Lafcadio Hearn and Natsume Soseki taught.

12. *Left:* A victim of leprosy photographed at the turn of the century graphically displaying the horrors of the disease.

13. *Below:* The magnificent flight of stone steps leading up to the Honmyoji temple, where Hannah first saw lepers.

14. *Facing page:* The Japan Church Missionary Society Conference of 1894, with Bishop Edward Bickersteth seated centre. Hannah, in the third row fifth from the right, is easily recognisable because of her height. On her left is Grace Nott, barely reaching Hannah's shoulder.

15. Ada Hannah Wright in 1897.

16. John Brandram

17. Mary Brandram

18. Katherine Tristram

19. Bishop Henry Evington

20. Albert Fuller

21. *Left:* Ada dressed in a kimono with two "Bible women."

22. *Below left:* A Japanese policeman accosted by a family of British tourists, as seen through the eyes of the French caricaturist Georges Bigot. Such encounters may have encouraged the Kumamoto chief of police to seek Hannah's assistance in instructing his officers in English.

23. *Below right:* Missionaries selling Testaments on a Japanese street in the 1900s.

24. *Facing page, above:* Hannah with fellow lady missionaries at Karuizawa.

25. *Facing page, below:* The main street of Karuizawa in the 1900s.

26, 27. Dr. Shunsuke Miyake and a nurse, Tamiko Mitsui, both of whom worked at the Kaishun Hospital for thirty years.

28. *Facing page, below:* The opening ceremony of the Kaishun Hospital on 12 November 1895. The two great antagonists, the Reverend John Brandram and Hannah, are seated in the middle, with Grace Nott beside Hannah and Bishop Henry Evington and the Reverend Archibald Hutchinson beside Brandram.

29. *Right:* Two young patients at the Kaishun Hospital.

30. *Below:* The laboratory surrounded by cherry trees donated to the hospital by Count Okuma in 1901.

31. Count Shigenobu Okuma, prominent statesman of the Meiji era and friend of Hannah.

32. Viscount Eiichi Shibusawa, banker, philanthropist, and supporter of the Kaishun Hospital.

33. The Bankers' Club, Tokyo, where Hannah gave her famous speech on behalf of the lepers of Japan.

34. Sir Claude MacDonald, said to have been won to Hannah's cause after a leper died at the gates of the British Embassy.

35. Hannah wearing the Medal of the Blue Ribbon, awarded by Emperor Meiji in 1906 for her services to lepers.

IMPERIAL HOTEL
TOKYO
THE HOME FOR TOURISTS
SOCIAL CENTER
OF THE CAPITAL

Asaku Sayashi
MANAGING DIRECTOR
IMPERIAL HOTEL IS THE ONLY
HOTEL IN JAPAN IN WHICH
THE CHIEF SHARE HOLDER I
H.I.J.M.'S HOUSEHOLD.

36. The Imperial Hotel, where Hannah often stayed during visits to Tokyo. Hannah justified this expediture by saying that only at such a prestigious address could she meet people rich and influential enough to support the hospital.

37. *Left:* Hannah's dogs waiting in a jinrikisha for their mistress to appear.

38. *Below:* Hannah's house at 436 Furushinyashiki.

39. *Facing page, above:* Malcolm, an American patient, who lived for many years at the hospital, sitting on his veranda.

40. *Facing page, below:* The Kaishun Hospital baseball team.

Base Ball Team.

41. A patient walking along the hospital avenue during the summer heat. A contemporary caption to this photograph noted that he was formerly a university professor.

42. Hannah in old age with a group of tennis-playing patients.

ed Christian leper had been enlisted as a future patient in the hope he would work hard to convert his fellow patients.

In the actual planning of the hospital, Hannah and her committee relied heavily on the advice of Dr. Teizo Iwai of the Red Cross Hospital in Tokyo. When the Iwakura Mission visited Geneva in 1873, its members had seen the Red Cross Society in its early stages and on their return to Japan had encouraged the development of a local branch. From its earliest days the Red Cross was strongly supported by the Imperial Family and quickly gained recognition throughout the country. The first Red Cross hospital in Japan was opened in Tokyo in 1891 and it was here that Dr. Iwai was working at the time Hannah consulted him. With the Sino-Japanese War of 1894–95 in full progress, Iwai must have been a busy man but he nevertheless found time to come up with a design that was filled with foresight and imagination although the whole concept of hospitals was still relatively new in late nineteenth-century Japan.

The first thing that struck visitors to the hospital was that it did not seem like a hospital at all. There was a building for the men and another for the women, designed to look much like an ordinary Japanese house. Each sunny and well-ventilated block had a row of four tatami rooms opening out onto a veranda. A larger building contained the consulting dispensary and waiting-room, kitchen, and offices. There was also a house for the doctor-superintendent, a bathhouse, and a storeroom. Between the buildings there was plenty of space for flowers and plants, while rising behind the hospital were woods of cedar and pine. Hannah received many gifts for the hospital, including an Estey organ (with three stops), two sets of silver for Holy Communion (two being necessary as the clergy could not drink from the same cup as the patients), a clock for the entrance, sixteen trees, and even a drainpipe to be used as a flower vase, presented by one of the workmen.

Despite much obvious goodwill, there were always problems. One obstacle Hannah had to overcome quickly, if she was going to retain what little CMS support she had, was her committee's reluctance to employ a Christian doctor-superintendent. In 1895 there cannot have been too many Japanese doctors who were both Christian and specialists in leprosy but fortunately one such man was found, a Dr. Tajiri. It was arranged that he would attend the hospital (for free) at least once a week and that an ordinary doctor, also a Christian, would live in the hospital as superintendent.

One important question taxing Hannah was what to name the hospital. She wanted to get away from the despair normally associated with the word leprosy and at the same time wanted to suggest a Christian influence. With the help of Professor Honda she settled on Kaishun. The English translation of this word, resurrection of hope, is a trifle heavy but the Japanese characters express more fully the concept of renewal at which Hannah was aiming.

The opening ceremony of the Kaishun Hospital took place on 12 November 1895. Henry Evington officiated, assisted by the Reverend John Brandram and Reverend Archibald Hutchinson. Only Christians were invited to the service but that evening some two hundred local villagers attended a magic-lantern show. Whatever misgivings the three English clergymen had over the venture were, for that day at least, suppressed. For Hannah the occasion marked the culmination of years of hard work and brought both her and her supporters deep gratification and joy.

15

Ada

The opening of the Kaishun Hospital was a remarkable feat. In stark contrast to so many of her missionary colleagues, Hannah had a solid achievement to her credit, one that made a real contribution to a real need and had been accomplished despite formidable difficulties. Professionally Hannah was busy and fulfilled but there remained a big gap in her life—Ada. She badly missed her niece and wanted her in Kumamoto as soon as possible. In May 1893 Hannah had concluded a letter to Crispian Fenn with a heartfelt plea:

> There is another matter very near to my heart which I should like to mention to you as Secretary for our Mission. My Niece, Ada Wright, is at "The Willows" waiting for Miss Schroder's permission to offer herself for Mission work. She is now 23 years old. The Archdeacon says he thinks that is the age at which candidates may offer. If she is permitted to offer this year, will you try to arrange that she comes to Japan? Archdeacon Warren says that if she does come, there can be no objection to her coming here to Miss Nott and I for the first year, while preparing for her language examination and after that she must go wherever the Conference places her. She would during that year have a far more practical insight into real Mission work, than is possible to obtain in Osaka. As it is, she could <u>now</u> do a great deal of work, if she were here! I should not be afraid in the least for her to

come, now, or even a year ago. If you can help me about her coming out, please do—she has belonged to me for so long.

Ada was the centre of Hannah's emotional life. More like a daughter than a niece, she also filled the roles of companion and secretary to her aunt, and it is not surprising that Hannah missed her deeply. Nearly three years, however, would pass before the two women were finally reunited. While Hannah was playing politics on behalf of her niece, Ada was studying at The Willows, the private college where the CMS sent many of their female candidates to be prepared for foreign service. Not gifted academically and for much of her life overshadowed by her powerful aunt, Ada nevertheless possessed distinctive qualities which enabled her to withstand considerable pressures and vicissitudes in later life. Although damningly described by Bishop Evington as "a nice quiet girl with no intellectual power"[1] on occasions she could display a determination and tenacity that must have surprised her detractors.

Her incentive to pass out of The Willows so that she could join her aunt and Grace Nott in Kumamoto was great. Hannah was not only Ada's entire family but also her mentor, guardian, and friend. True, Ada did have a brother, Samuel, but from the complete absence of any reference to him in her diaries or papers except the record of his death, it would seem they were not close. Ada was exceptionally pretty and sweet-natured, and it is hard to believe that she did not attract the attentions of young men. But the evidence suggests that her aunt did not approve of sex in any form, and such attitudes must have rubbed off on the impressionable Ada. At any rate no romantic attachments appear to have stood in the way of Ada's ambition to join her aunt as a CMS missionary, only the intransigence of the system.

The Willows was a large Victorian house in north London not far from the men's missionary college in Islington. Set in eleven acres of green grass and surrounded by majestic trees, The Willows was about as far removed from the realities of the mission field in Africa or India as is possible to imagine. By coincidence, the school's founder, Catherine Pennefather, had lived in Barnet for the first nine years of Hannah's life as the wife of the Anglican vicar and must have known the Riddell family. Indeed, devoted as she was to the CMS and the YMWCA, she may well have had an early influence on Hannah.

Catherine Pennefather perfectly embodied the Victorian ideals of

Christian womanhood, as is illustrated by this gem of an anecdote, dripping with saccharine and quoted in Mrs. Pennefather's obituary in the 1893 April edition of *India's Women:*

> Catherine's . . . chief delight was in the beautiful garden. Here the sweet flowers peeped out of their shy eyes at her, and she smiled at them and loved them. The birds and insects were her friends to whom she whispered her secrets. One day a bee buzzed round the little girl and left his sting in her tiny hand. She felt the pain but did not know what it was and running to her mother, exclaimed, "Mamma, mamma, a little bee came on my hand and kissed it too hard."

Life for Ada at The Willows was agreeable enough. There was plenty of companionship, the surroundings were soothing, and the days not too arduous. Much of the women's time was spent in Bible study. When Ada was there in 1893, the timetable included daily scripture lessons with instruction on difficult passages once a week from the Reverend Gordon Calthrop and on Sundays an hour's Bible study with Miss E. S. Elliott.

The candidates also learned as much as they could about the special problems and achievements of the different missions. There was a weekly lesson in book-keeping to prepare them for taking charge of mission finances, lessons in cooking for invalids, and a weekly drill in tonic sol-fa, presumably to ensure they could sing hymns in tune. Other activities included visiting the poor in local neighbourhoods and some basic medical training.

In view of the fact that many of these ladies had led very sheltered lives but were now bound for such far-flung and difficult places, it is surprising that the CMS did not make medical training a higher priority. In fact, the CMS seems to have been generally wary of putting too much emphasis on the medical skills of its women missionaries. The following makes the society's chief objective clear:

> Two of the above [candidates] have the additional qualification of being fully trained hospital nurses. We speak of this as an "additional" qualification, for it is not one which will do instead of any other qualifications that the ordinary missionary needs. If a nurse becomes a missionary her one object must be the winning of souls. Her

work is not only nursing; she must be able to explain the Gospel of Christ to her patients in their own language, and she needs to be as skilled in dealing with sin-stricken souls as she is in relieving bodily pain.[2]

This statement of policy was reflected in John Brandram's and Henry Evington's tepid reactions to Hannah's urgent desire to bring relief to the lepers. The message was unequivocal—medical work was acceptable for opening doors and as an adjunct to a missionary's work but must not be allowed to get in the way of pure evangelism.

Ada had the habit of making jottings in her *Day Book of Religious Sayings* which are tantalisingly brief. When these entries start in 1892, she was already a student at The Willows and was to remain based there until she was finally accepted by the society in the summer of 1896. Life was not all hard work. During these years her notes mention friends and outings but she obviously longed for the day when her "offer" would be accepted and she could sail for Japan.

Ada received a setback in November 1893, when she caught influenza and spent that Christmas in hospital. She must have been seriously ill because it was not until 30 April 1894 that she left the cottage hospital (close to The Willows) and returned to the college. At the end of May she saw Dr. Tirard, consulting physician to the society. On 4 June she had an interview with the medical board, then a series of interviews with various important figures in the CMS hierarchy, and on 24 September a final examination by the society's doctors. Three days later came dire news. Ada's "offer" to the CMS had been rejected. While the immediate reasons given for this failure were medical, it is clear from the minutes of the Ladies Consultative Committee that apart from her health problems there had also been doubts about Ada's suitability for work in the foreign field.

Ada spent the next few months in Devon, perhaps in an effort to restore her health. She also appears to have lived in Brighton for a large part of 1895, making frequent trips to Dorking and to The Willows, where she no doubt worked hard to ensure success at her next attempt to become a missionary.

By mid April 1896, Ada's luck finally began to improve. There was another examination by Dr. Tirard and more interviews, including one with the sympathetic Baring Baring-Gould, who had replaced Fenn as secretary to the CMS with responsibility for Japan. He was also a friend and supporter of Hannah and Grace who knew very well how much they wanted Ada to join them. In a letter he wrote to Grace dated 29 April 1896 came the news Hannah had been waiting so long to hear:

> You will both be pleased to know that yesterday Miss Riddell's niece was "accepted as a candidate" by the committee. She will I hope be sent to a clergyman for a few weeks in order that she may have individual attention in the study of her Bible in which at present she is not very strong. And then I cherish the <u>hope</u> that in October she may be allowed to start for Kumamoto. Should this be the case it will simplify your plans, I imagine, for your furlough.

Ada's relief and joy at being at last accepted leaps off the page in her letter to the Reverend D. H. D. Wilkinson:

> I can't tell you how very thankful I am, for it is such an honour to be allowed to go and tell the heathen of "Jesus and His love." I feel how utterly unworthy I am and how weak, but HE has promised to perfect His strength in my weakness.

Ada left no record of the preparations for her departure but May Freeth, a fellow student at The Willows who was to spend the next forty-odd years in Kyushu as a missionary, had left for Japan nine months earlier, and in long letters written home to Ireland gives a vivid impression of a young missionary's last few days in England. There were many practical matters to consider and the Lay Secretary, D. M. Lang, whose son was posted to Kumamoto at the same time as Hannah and Grace, was on hand to give advice. He thought one hundred pounds should be enough money for a year but if May wanted to transfer money from home it could be done through the Hong Kong and Shanghai Bank at any time. She was strongly advised <u>not</u> to be too economical and <u>not</u> to try and do without luxuries but to consider her health and comfort first. All female missionaries had someone on the ladies' consultative committee to whom they could write as a friend when they were abroad about little things "they might not like to trouble the men with." There were emotional goodbyes to be said to friends and to Miss Schroder, principal of The Willows. And it was, of course, essential to have a formal photograph taken to give to family and friends. (Austen's of Highbury gave special rates to Willowites.)

On 29 September Ada was issued with her official instructions from the CMS:

> You, dear Miss Wright, the Committee have sincere pleasure in sending forth to be associated—in the first instance, should the Conference approve—with your Aunt, Miss Riddell, and Miss Nott, in their work at Kumamoto. They heartily thank God for the marked spiritual results which have crowned their sisters' labours in that place, and especially in connexion with the Leper Hospital. You have had the opportunity of enjoying an unusual length of time in preparing for Foreign Service, and have passed through a very varied experience of work; and though the period has sometimes doubtless appeared to you unduly prolonged, the Committee cannot but believe that all through your missionary career you will heartily thank God for having thus equipped you for his service in the Foreign Field. Experience has been gained, character has been strengthened, knowledge has been acquired, and a mental and moral discipline has been passed through which with the Divine blessing will prove rich in fruitfulness in your future life. Whenever located at Kumamoto you will need to be carefully on your guard lest your sympathies and interest become so bound up with the Hospital that it claims an undue share of your strength and time; and it will require no little self-control and sanctified common-sense so to adjust your time as to devote a due proportion to more general evangelistic work among your sisters in Japan. Perhaps too, it is not unneedful to warn you against becoming so absorbed with various kinds of work at the outset of your Missionary life as to leave an inadequate amount of time for the study of the language. Until you have passed your examinations let the Vernacular be the first claim upon all your energies. Above all the Committee would urge you to remember that, as was so well said at a recent Conference in Japan, your success as a missionary depends entirely upon the closeness of your walk with the Divine Master. Be assured you leave in England very many who will follow you with the supplication of the Apostle for his Philippian converts: "This I pray that your love may abound yet more and more in knowledge and in all judgement: that

ye may approve things that are excellent, that ye may be sincere and without offence till the day of Christ; being filled with the fruits of righteousness which are by Jesus Christ unto the glory and grace of God" [Phil. 10: 9–11].[3]

This stern document signed by Baring-Gould and another secretary to the CMS, F. Baylis, contained a clear warning to Ada that had a familiar ring to it. The CMS was nothing if not consistent. The leper hospital was all very well as long as it did not get in the way of Ada's main work, which was to learn the language and convert Japanese souls to the Christian faith as speedily as possible.

On the evening of 29 September the missionaries were formally "dismissed" at Exeter Hall in London. The *Times* of 30 September 1896 gave the occasion full coverage under the headline "Ecclesiastical Intelligence":

Exeter Hall was crowded last night upon the occasion of a public farewell to missionaries about to proceed to Egypt, Palestine, Ceylon, China, Japan, and British Columbia under the auspices of the Church Missionary Society. Sir John H. Kenaway, MP, president of the society, took the chair and said the occasion was a very solemn one, a new departure of British missionaries to the work that lay before them in various parts of the world. The times in which we lived were solemn also, and there was much anxiety and difficulty as the 19th century drew to a close . . . Two sovereigns, in the meantime, whose territories united would cover a third of the inhabited globe, and who were knit together by ties of kinship and affection, were dwelling under the same roof, and a few hours before were worshipping together in a humble Scottish kirk . . . The Chairman bade a cordial farewell and God-speed to the missionaries. The Reverend Henry Fox, the Honourary Secretary of the Church Missionary Society, stated that in all 149 missionaries were going abroad in the course of the next few months, of whom seventy-one were returning missionaries, and seventy-eight were going out for the first time. Of the latter eight were going out on their own charges, six would be supported by the colonial associations, and fifty-seven had been appropriated as their missionaries by individual members of the society.

Like May Freeth, Ada spent her last few nights in England in Black-heath, south London, where the CMS owned a number of houses at which missionaries could lodge when they were home on leave. Then at last, after all the years of preparation and anticipation, on 9 October 1896 Ada set sail on the SS *Australia* for Nagasaki. She was not alone. Travelling with her was the new Bishop of Hokkaido, the Reverend P. K. Fyson, and his wife, Miss Edith Bryant, Miss Annie Carr, and Miss Beatrice Nottidge. On 24 November Ada arrived in Nagasaki to be reunited with her beloved aunt.

CHAPTER 16

Conflict

Nagasaki was the CMS headquarters in Kyushu and the residence of Bishop Henry Evington. One of Bishop Bickersteth's initiatives had been the establishment of bishoprics in Hokkaido and Kyushu, which, given the elongated geography of Japan, made a good deal of administrative sense. Evington, a hardworking, orthodox missionary with long experience in the field, was a natural choice to fill the new job in Kyushu and took up office in 1894.

That same year other events took place that were to influence the lives of the small band of CMS missionaries in Kyushu. Of international significance was the outbreak of war between Japan and China over their respective interests in Korea, which led to thousands of troops pouring through Kumamoto on their way to and from the front. Western observers often commented on the soldiers' quiet and orderly behaviour, and the missionaries made the most of their new opportunities to evangelise among them.

Hannah recounted how she herself went to the preaching hall in Kumamoto, where for months servicemen had been quartered, to play the organ. She had watched the veranda slowly fill up with soldiers and had later presented them with a number of Bibles. Shortly after they had started for the war, she had a letter from four of them telling her how they met each day to read the New Testament together. Another letter soon came describing in graphic detail how they had taken Port Arthur.

During the war, permission was given to distribute Bibles to soldiers, and for the first time Christian preachers were allowed to become army chaplains. On the domestic front, there was an immediate improvement in the missionaries' lives when, in September 1894, passport requirements were eased as a result of an Anglo-Japanese agreement that heralded the end of the unequal treaties. The more liberal rules meant the missionaries could hold passports which were valid for a year, a change that allowed them to travel anywhere in Japan. Apart from the obvious logistical advantages of the new passports, the agreement also did much to blunt the long-standing Japanese resentment of the part the British played in the unequal treaties.

Before Henry Evington went back to England for consecration, he spent eleven months in Kumamoto substituting for Brandram, who was on leave in England. He and Hannah, therefore, had plenty of opportunity to get to know one another, but it was an association doomed to failure. The problem was rooted in Hannah's attitude to authority, particularly her relationship with Brandram, whom she clearly regarded as ineffectual, lacking strength of character and imagination. What is more, Brandram had not given the hospital project the whole-hearted support she felt it deserved.

In fact, John Brandram was a kind and deeply spiritual man who had lived through difficult times and was already showing symptoms of the illness that eventually killed him. It was thus an unfortunate twist of fate that brought together these two very different personalities in such close circumstances. In the small missionary community in which they lived, such rifts were not easily concealed and inevitably those involved took sides.

There was no question as to whom Henry Evington supported: "I would rather lose Miss R from my diocese twice or three times than Mr. B once."[1] But Hannah did at least have one firm ally in Grace Nott, who proved to be as unswerving in her determination to build the leper hospital as Hannah herself. Grace gave Hannah a clear vote of confidence when she wrote in her first annual report that not least of God's mercies was that He had called her and Hannah to the same station and allowed them to be fellow workers.

When Hannah introduced Ada to Bishop Evington in Nagasaki in late November 1896, relations between them were strained. No doubt the niceties were observed but Evington later recorded how he had on that occasion called them both into his study and given Ada a stern lecture on the importance of throwing all her energies into the study of the language. No wonder Hannah and her niece did not dally long in Nagasaki. Four days after arriving in Japan, Ada finally reached Kumamoto.

Once installed in Choanji-cho, despite the protection of her aunt and Grace, Ada soon discovered that Japan was a very different place from any she had previously encountered. As she pointed out a little forlornly in her first report to the CMS in 1897, "Especially do we need prayer and guidance, not only in the way of working and speaking but also in the way of daily living, for the point of view of the people of this country is so widely different from anything one has experience of at home."

Though problems remained, Hannah was able to produce a glowing progress report on the early days of the hospital. Dr. Shunsuke Miyake had taken over from Dr. Tajiri and was proving a great success. As he had studied under Dr. Baelz in Tokyo, Miyake's medical qualifications were excellent; what is more, he was an earnest Christian. There were twenty-four patients in the hospital, and they managed all the gardening and sweeping themselves. Their living arrangements were organised to make them as self-supporting as possible. For instance, a lame patient would be quartered with one who could walk but had lost the use of his hands. Ten of the twenty-four patients were Christian.

But success breeds its own problems and, writing to the CMS about a year after the hospital had opened, Hannah produced a lengthy shopping list. She wanted one hundred pounds for a new men's ward, a schoolroom, an isolation ward, a nurses' home, and operating room, not to mention a microscope.

Although the hospital was obviously Hannah's chief priority, in her formal report to the CMS, she was careful to emphasise her other missionary work. She had not been idle. Amongst all her other activities, Hannah had found the time to publish (with the help of Japanese friends) a Japanese translation of the *Daily Light,* which, she claimed, had been bought enthusiastically by missionaries of all denominations.

On the face of it, Hannah was a model lady missionary, but after the opening of the Kaishun Hospital her relations with her fellow missionaries grew steadily worse. She was undoubtedly strong meat for genteel Victorian tastes, and most of her immediate colleagues were nothing if not deeply and conservatively entrenched in the social conventions of their day. Many of them sought to ease the physical and cultural gulf between Britain and Japan by simply transferring their English lifestyle, complete with all its trappings, to their mission post.

On this subject May Freeth's letters are revealing. She was highly intelligent, well educated, and in her long years in Japan accomplished a great deal. For most of her career she lived a simple, hard-working life among Japanese people. But her early letters home, written in the mid 1890s when she was posted in Fukuoka, portray the Kyushu missionary circle as a comfortable microcosm of Victorian society.

In a letter to her sister dated 9 February 1897 May wrote, "I am trying to make myself a new silk blouse. I must have an evening one to go to Nagasaki with because we have to make ourselves smart for Mrs. Evington's 'at home.'" Of a similar engagement she had attended some months earlier she wrote, "The Bishop and Mrs. Evington had an at home that evening. We had lots of music and it was so nice. Mr. Painter has a lovely tenor voice and though you may laugh, it was a real treat to see someone in really nice evening dress again. The clergymen always wear their clericals." May also wrote of how she had been teaching eighteen-year-old girls "the three R's with a vengeance. I had Roman History and Rhetoric and, Ethel, Revelation!!! Did you ever hear of teaching Japanese such stuff? I pitied them with all my heart."

The missionaries were generally decent people, utterly convinced of the rightness of their cause. But they rarely questioned their own values and often, if unconsciously, showed condescension and pity for the "heathen" among whom they had chosen to live. In an uncharacteristic outburst of irritation at the limited intellectual world inhabited by some of her colleagues, the normally charitable May wrote to her sister from Nagasaki, where she had spent Christmas with the British Consul:

> You can't think what a treat it is to be amongst men again and to hear a little outside talk about present-day events, books, etc. Mrs. Hutchinson [wife of the CMS priest in Fukuoka] is of course different but the women missionaries seem to have so little to talk about and to have read so little. Ethel has never even read any Shakespeare though she has begun a little now on my recommendation. There seems so much silly talk when a lot of women get together. I know I am as bad because I find it very difficult to keep up to date in things and one has so little time for reading. I often wonder what good my education is. I seem to be forgetting everything I ever

knew. I don't want to be conceited but no other girl in this island has had anything like the education I have had and they seem to get on well enough without it.

The experience of another culture did not often lead the missionaries to look afresh at their own, but it was through them that many Japanese, especially in the rural parts of the country, had their first encounters with the West. And there were undoubtedly numerous mutual benefits from that contact. In another letter May gave a charming description of a party she held for some Japanese ladies:

We had a very pleasant time indeed and I think everyone enjoyed themselves. Only about 32 came as several had head colds, but the room was well filled. We began with a hymn, then the 103rd Psalm was read, followed by a short prayer and another hymn. Then we had tea and cakes . . . After tea we gave them all a cracker each and that created a good deal of amusement. There were only caps and puzzles inside them, but some of the old ladies put the caps on and looked so funny. Although they came soon after seven it must have been 8:30 when we began to play. We had cat and mouse, which they thoroughly enjoyed. Osumi-san made us all laugh very much when she was the mouse. She crouched down and went about squeaking and looked so ridiculous, she was active too. Then they all tried to pin on the donkey's tail blindfold . . . For the last game we collected all the chairs in the house and had musical chairs to finish up with.

Despite sharing many of her fellow missionaries' values and aspirations, Hannah did not fit happily into their cosy world, a fact that was clear from the outset. Finding herself in a foreign land, surrounded by challenges, she was able to develop her talents in a way that would have been very much more difficult in England. Knowing her own capabilities and having tested them with the successful launching of the Kaishun Hospital, she found the restraints imposed upon her by her missionary superiors increasingly difficult to accept. Equally, they considered her outspokenness, independence, and working methods both disruptive and disquieting.

17

Battle Lines

In the autumn of 1898 Bishop Evington gave vent to his feelings about Hannah in a letter written to Baring-Gould which, coming from a man of the cloth, is extraordinarily venomous. He began by saying how disappointed he was that Hannah was not returning to England for her furlough. As with most aspects of missionary life, the CMS had firm rules about home leave, rules which Hannah, in her typical manner, sought to circumnavigate.

Working by the book, she should have returned to England in 1897 with Grace Nott. But knowing that in their combined absence, there was no one competent or interested enough to run the hospital, she had persuaded Dr. Maurice Paul in Nagasaki to give her a certificate confirming the excellent state of her health and granting her a two-year extension. Unfortunately she then promptly became seriously ill with peritonitis followed by blood poisoning and was out of action for much of 1897 and 1898.

Evington desperately wanted Hannah out of Kumamoto because he felt her continued presence there would result in John Brandram having a complete breakdown. Brandram had shown symptoms of becoming unhinged as early as the spring of 1897 and had become even worse during the summer, apparently leaving for the hills in a most excited state. May Freeth's letters of this period allude to the problem: "Mrs. Brandram is kind enough to say that I have done her good. There has been a good deal of trouble here lately, not amongst the heathen but difficulties amongst the Christians and the Brandrams have been a good deal troubled and anxious about it all."

May Freeth also reported that in April Brandram had turned up unexpectedly in Fukuoka:

> We were very much astonished by the arrival of Mr. Brandram. He had come from Kumamoto the night before with the Bishop, who had ordered him off for a few days' change and rest. There has been some trouble at Kumamoto lately and Mr. Brandram has had a rather anxious time and from want of sleep etc. was tired out so he came round to ask us to take him for a good walk to tire his body. He wouldn't take any excuse . . . and he said it was our duty because if he didn't sleep, he would go cracked.

In his letter to Baring-Gould, Bishop Evington blamed Hannah unequivocally for Brandram's disturbed state of mind. And should he lose Brandram, Evington made it clear that he would not be able to replace him because none of his senior missionaries was prepared to work alongside Hannah in Kumamoto.

He went on to complain bitterly that the leper hospital had a "glamour" around it far beyond the proportion it occupied in the work of the mission, while the effort among the women had been largely neglected since Grace Nott's departure. The gloves were off, and in this letter which burns with resentment, Evington makes patently clear his attitude to the Kaishun Hospital: "So long as the hospital workers are made to take a secondary place and act as a handmaid to the Evangelistic work, I shall be glad to see it prosper: if however it interferes with the proper work I shall feel bound to oppose it and doubtless I can do so."

Warming to his theme, Evington reported that he had been told several times that Hannah had been disloyal to him and that he now believed her to be "not true." Realising that this was tantamount to calling her a liar, he quickly (but unconvincingly) added that he was sure any duplicity was not intentional, merely the result of habit.

The bishop had a lot to get off his chest but was by no means finished. He next turned to Hannah's lifestyle, which was certainly a cut above that of most missionaries. From where, he wondered did she get her money? Someone had remarked to him that Miss Riddell must have plenty of it, judging from the lavish picnics she hosted in the summer mountain resort at Karuizawa, not to mention the chair and four coolies she had in attendance every day. Evington described her claim of fifty yen for additional medical expenses "a prostitution" of CMS funds and gave a sinister warning that, should the claim be granted, it would lead to something more than unpleasantness, possibly both to Miss Riddell and also to the society.

Yet another grievance ventilated by the bishop in this letter concerned Ada. He had obviously never expected her to pass her Japanese exam, which was why he had given her such a clear warning, in Hannah's presence, about putting all her efforts into studying the language. From what he had seen with Miss Nott "'Auntie' would have 101 little errands," and Ada's study would have to take second place to Hannah's demands. Evington described Ada as "one who had all the individuality crushed out of her by a weighty personality" and quoted an acquaintance who had said she thought Ada would be much better living away from her aunt, though it would be treason to say so.

While much of the bishop's criticism of Hannah may have been unfair and stemmed from his personal dislike of her, on one aspect of her behaviour, at least, he was completely accurate: "The power which this lady possesses of getting round people is wonderful and she knows it." He went on to deplore her habit of writing directly to the parent committee in London over the heads of the local Kyushu authorities whenever she wanted to achieve a particular objective, though acknowledging that she was extraordinarily plausible and persuasive.

The case of a Mrs. Kitahara is a perfect illustration of the intense irritation Hannah caused her colleagues by taking an independent line without first consulting them. She had decided that Mrs. Kitahara, the wife of a leper, should go to Osaka to be trained as a "Bible woman," a woman who taught the basics of Christianity to her fellow Japanese. The problem was that Hannah had promised Mrs. Kitahara a place in the training school before formally applying to Brandram and the Kyushu conference.

Whatever the merits of the case, the Reverend Archibald Hutchinson, in Fukuoka, was not going to be pushed around by Hannah Riddell. In a letter to London he recommended Mrs. Kitahara's application be refused on the grounds that, as the wife of a leper, she would have little access to Japanese households and that even if she were living apart from her husband, she would be surrounded by suspicion and fear. Hutchinson may have been right but his viewpoint was hardly that of a humanitarian. He added gratuitously that "a wife's duties are by a sick husband and no agreement can override a husband's right to summon his wife to his side, whenever he wishes." Hutchinson expressed the firm opinion that it would be wrong to risk CMS funds on the training and support of Mrs. Kitahara so long as her husband was alive.

Interestingly John Brandram, traditionally cast in the role of Hannah's chief interlocutor, was clearly bothered by Hutchinson's hard line, pointing out that Mrs. Kitahara's application had, in fact, been supported by both the Japanese workers' committee and a doctor and remarking that if her application were refused, the church would be losing a good worker. It is difficult not to sympathise with Brandram, caught as he was between stubborn and powerful forces. Little wonder that he felt on this occasion unable to vote, merely saying that he gladly left the decision on this difficult question in the hands of his brethren.

It is worth looking at the sad little saga of Mrs. Kitahara in some detail because it so vividly encapsulates the increasingly fraught situation that had developed within the small Christian community in Kyushu. On the one side was Hannah, raring to go, full of ideas and energy but woefully lacking tact and diplomacy in the handling of her colleagues. On the other side were ranged the conservative forces of the CMS, determined to win souls but only through correct channels and by orthodox procedures. Somewhere in the middle of all this were the Japanese, who must at times have found the behaviour of the English missionaries distinctly odd.

Despite all these tensions, there is evidence that the example of the Kaishun Hospital had stirred the conscience of Japanese officialdom. In the spring of 1898 John Brandram was approached by several army doctors stationed with the garrison, who expressed the wish to do something for the poor in Kumamoto. They had been advised that a dispensary would be of great benefit to the city. But because the doctors were soldiers and always subject to transfer at short notice, they wanted the dispensary run by the Christian churches in Kumamoto to ensure continuity. The missionaries were delighted. Brandram and Hannah conferred (perfectly amicably it would seem, at least on this occasion) and came up with a plan. The army doctors would do all the work but be under the control of the two doctors at the Kaishun Hospital and ultimately under the management of Hannah. Brandram would be responsible only for evangelistic work, an arrangement that would suit him very well. He even gave Hannah a plug, saying that not only was she willing to undertake the work but would do it very well. For this project, perhaps because it had the firm backing of Brandram, CMS funds were available and a grant of sixty pounds per annum was produced from the medical auxiliary.

From the London perspective, CMS work in Kumamoto was progressing in a satisfactory manner and Hannah's contribution could not be denied. What, then, were they to make of Bishop Evington's bomb-shell? In his final broadside, Evington let forth some powerful prose, leaving no *t* uncrossed nor *i* undotted:

> It is now simply the fact that one of our stations is suffering silently but very deeply and that the cause must sooner or later burst forth to the light and end in bitterness and exposure. We have strong-minded ladies, self-willed ones, perhaps in the mission field and ladies who want to carry out their own crotchets, but we have no other in Kyushu of whom we feel that she is not true and is guilty of circumvention to accomplish her object.

Baring-Gould's reaction to this vitriolic letter is not recorded but he would surely have received it with dismay. His own frequent letters to Hannah are always filled with warmth and concern for her health and welfare. He had shown a keen interest in the hospital and although he had sometimes echoed the official view about not letting it take up too much of the mission's time, he had been an enthusiastic supporter, even sending money out of his own pocket to the hospital fund. Hannah was a friend of the family and a visitor at his house, and he seems to have taken a particular interest in her missionary career from its start. But Henry Evington's letter could hardly be ignored. And it was, after all, merely explicit confirmation of disturbing rumblings that had been reaching London for a long while.

In fact, the parent committee had already decided to recall Hannah and had sent the mission secretary, Albert Fuller, a telegram concerning her on 13 September. "Health demands return" was a directive she had managed to duck, thanks to Dr. Paul, who had firmly advised her not to leave for England until the spring. However, stung into action by the bishop's letter, the parent committee despatched a second, more urgent telegram to Fuller in December, with the brief message "Riddell return promptly convinced important." Fuller was away when the cable arrived and it was opened by Henry Evington, who immediately concluded that this order was the result of his own action and embarked on some gentle backpedalling. He wrote to Baring-Gould, saying that as Hannah's passage was now booked for 25 March, he thought it unnecessary to accelerate her departure.

Furthermore, the temperature in Kumamoto seemed to have cooled. On a recent visit Evington had found Brandram less agitated on the subject of Hannah, merely remarking that "she gets bigger every day, the last move is that she has joined the Ladies Club in London."[1] That Hannah should have been censured for simply joining a club seems a little hard. But living as she did in a society that was strongly conscious of background, perhaps she was sometimes the target of such invective because she was so clearly socially ambitious. On her last encounter with Evington, Hannah had even gone so far as to apologise for some unflattering comment she had made about him, adding that she had always held him in great affection, a remark which Evington records "made me feel somewhat otherwise than joyed."[2]

If Hannah was trying to mend fences, it was too late. When she finally saw the telegram herself, she must have realised something was seriously amiss and that the cable had been prompted by more than just concern for her health. But after a heated correspondence between Hannah and London, it was agreed that she should stick to her original plan and leave Japan on 25 March. Hannah had achieved her objective. By the time she sailed for England, Grace Nott would be back in Kumamoto. Ada would not therefore be left abandoned and, most important of all, the reins of the hospital would be in safe hands.

The dramas going on behind the scenes do not seem to have affected Hannah's work, and she wrote a particularly full report for 1898. Written in December, the report gives a touching description of Christmas in the hospital. Each patient received a cushion, whose cover had been embroidered in England by supporters of the hospital. The patients sat on their new cushions before the Christmas tree, which was a great novelty. There were presents for everyone. A ten-dollar donation had been spent on useful items decided upon by two specially formed committees. These gifts were given out with an amusing present such as a bunch of carrots and a clever pun.

Hannah was never short of new ideas. That Christmas she inaugurated a "Christmas Bank" into which Japanese could deposit any sum up to a dollar and even earn a little interest. They were not allowed to take it out until the following 20 December, the objective being to help them save for New Year expenses.

At the same time that Hannah was embattled over her furlough plans, yet another drama was unfolding, this one around Ada. Safe under the protection of her aunt and Grace Nott, Ada had nevertheless found it difficult to get herself established since her arrival in Japan. Her first annual report says it all: "At present one is so utterly helpless, everything is so new, and one feels so out of it all in not being able to understand or speak a single word; and yet every one is so kind in doing all they can to make one feel more at home and by degrees we begin to find our feet, though it takes a long, long time, with a great deal of prayer for patience and perseverance."

Ada had managed a little work here and there, playing the organ at the Kaishun Hospital and helping out with Sunday school but had achieved little of substance. But achievement was not important in her first year, as she was expected to devote most of her time to studying Japanese. By no means a gifted linguist at the best of times, Ada had received a further set-back when her aunt became ill only six months after she arrived. With Grace in England, Ada alone was on hand to help and was no doubt kept busy day and night nursing Hannah and doing those "101 little errands" to which Evington had sarcastically referred.

The truth was that by the end of 1898, Ada was ill-prepared for her first language examination despite the fact she had already been in Japan two years and the examination was normally taken after only one. Hannah must have seen the writing on the wall and could not resist meddling. After Ada had departed for Nagasaki to take the dreaded exam, Hannah wrote to Evington—an unwise decision. Up to her old tricks, she tried to work round the system by telling Evington that however badly Ada did in her exam she, Hannah, was satisfied she could pass and any failure on Ada's part was purely the result of nerves and having so devotedly nursed her aunt (thus, incidentally saving the CMS money). Such arguments were not likely to influence Hannah's two most powerful antagonists, Evington and Fuller, who also happened to be Ada's examiners.

It is hardly surprising that she failed miserably. A detailed report of the exam survives, and it is clear that it was a formidable test:

<u>Written Grammar</u>. There was a bad failure in this important sub-
ject. Some parts shewed ignorance extending beyond that of the
Japanese Language.

The result of the attempt to translate brief passages from the
Gospels into Colloquial Japanese was suggestive of a first effort.

There was ignorance of words, general lack of readiness, and a
great want of accuracy in the knowledge of particles and tenses.

In conversation the same lack of definite knowledge was mani-
fest.[3]

With her letter to Evington Hannah had succeeded only in making a
bad situation worse. Fuller, who comes across as a cold and distant man—
May Freeth said he had "very bad delivery"—was furious and in a letter to
Baring-Gould pours scorn on Hannah's naïve intervention. Of Ada he
could say only "she is extremely nice and good, but all who know her out
here feel that her mental power is exceedingly small and I am bound to
add that the general opinion is that she is not up to the standard needed
for Japan . . . it is our opinion that she should be recalled."

There followed the comments of the other senior Kyushu missionaries.
James Hind, the CMS missionary in Kokura, fully agreed with Fuller,
while Hutchinson thought she should be transferred rather than recalled
since the latter word implied spiritual deficiency. Brandram, as usual, sat
on the fence, refusing to come down firmly on one side or the other. He
lamented that Ada would always be a nonentity if she remained under
her aunt's shadow. And although it seemed cruel to vote for her recall he
felt it would save money to do so.

Despite all that Hannah had achieved in her first eight years in Japan,
by the beginning of 1899 the outlook for her and Ada was bleak. Although they may not have realised it at the time, when they said farewell
to one another on 25 March, the day Hannah set sail for England, they
faced a very uncertain future.

18

Defeat

Before leaving Nagasaki, Hannah received an unwelcome visitor in the shape of Bishop Henry Evington on board the German ship that was to carry her to England. On meeting her, Evington informed Hannah that the telegram summoning her home had been sent as a result of a letter he had written. The ensuing conversation was, Evington recorded, a most painful one. Hannah was apparently astonished to learn that there had been so much concern over her relationship with Brandram and gave the bishop a very different version of events.

Perhaps worried that he had gone too far, Evington later admitted to Baring-Gould that he felt he had acted very cruelly during his meeting with Hannah and confessed that, at times, it seemed as if they were strong men opposing a defenceless woman. And at least on one point he had come away from Kumamoto satisfied: Evington had been troubled about the lack of proper accounts for the hospital. (Did he perhaps think that Hannah had been dipping into the till?) But Evington noted that indeed the accounts were satisfactory and added that the able and economical way the institution had been managed had impressed him. At last, it seems, Hannah had done something right.

On 17 March, shortly before Hannah embarked on the voyage home, the ladies consultative committee had met in London. One item on the agenda had been to consider Ada's case in light of the less than flattering report received from the Kyushu conference. After prayer for guidance, the group came up with a commendably fair decision. The women's consensus was that since it had been their decision to send Ada to Japan in the first place, they must take some of the responsibility for any failure. They also acknowledged that owing to Hannah's illness Ada might not have had enough time to study Japanese. They therefore granted her a six-month extension, with the proviso that if she failed again, she should be withdrawn from Japan. Finally, they added that if she remained in Japan, she should serve in a different place from her aunt.

Hannah arrived in England in late May and for three months is lost to sight. After eight years' absence from England, she must have been busy catching up with friends and would have been particularly anxious to see the Baring-Goulds and other senior figures in the CMS to express her side of the Kyushu dispute. And she would have wasted no time in campaigning for support for the Kaishun Hospital.

Hannah re-emerges in a letter written to the Reverend Henry Fox, the new CMS secretary responsible for Japan. This letter, dated 20 September 1899, makes it clear that Hannah and Fox had recently met and Hannah had been unequivocally confronted with her Kyushu colleagues' accusations: "I am so afraid lest I should have seemed in word or manner to be out of charity with my fellow missionaries. I do hope not—for though I cannot help but be very very hurt by such degrading as well as painful statements I do acquit them of knowing what they are doing."

Five months later (events were clearly not moving fast), on 19 February 1900, the parent committee met to consider among other items the personnel problems in Kumamoto. The members decided to avoid a final decision on the issue and merely approved a draft letter to Fuller. They were no doubt influenced by Baring-Gould, who, still batting for Hannah, had written to them, pointing out the grave consequences of Hannah's withdrawal from Kumamoto. Baring-Gould noted that her departure would result in the entire break-up of the hospital because no one else was capable of running it, and thus the CMS would lose an important influence "exerted on the high class of Japanese generally." Significantly there is no mention of the effect closure would have had on the patients. "All however that I earnestly pray for," wrote Baring-Gould with a final flourish, "is that absolutely impartial justice may be dealt out to accusers and accused."

Meanwhile, back in Japan, Ada was sorting out her own future. It is not recorded whether she attempted the exam for the third time and failed or if she simply never tried, unable perhaps to face the prospect of yet another humiliating encounter with Fuller and Evington. In any case, by the spring of 1900 it was evident that Ada and the CMS would have to part company. The CMS might have transferred Ada to another country but Ada, anxious not to have to try to learn yet another new language and having no ties in England, desperately wanted to remain in Japan.

Ada was not without her supporters, and soon her Japanese Christian friends were working hard to find her alternative employment in the mission field. In the end, it was the energetic and loyal Professor Honda who came up with the solution. He had himself been offered the job of principal to the American Episcopal Girls School in Tokyo and to his surprise had received permission from the government to accept the post.

The American missionaries' sphere of influence was north of Tokyo and their bishop was a lively and personable man called John McKim. Honda affected an introduction between Ada and McKim and before long she had been offered a job with the Americans in Maebashi on a year's probation. On 18 May the CMS accepted Ada's resignation. She evidently bore them no grudge. Typically, in her letter of resignation to Fuller, she thanked him for all the trouble he had taken and asked how much of her furniture allowance she should return.

Two months before the CMS received Ada's resignation, Fuller was passing to London documents concerning Grace Nott's intention to leave the CMS. Exactly why Grace decided to quit the society at this juncture is open to speculation since she made it clear to Fuller she did not wish to discuss the matter. Her widowed mother was elderly and it is likely that Grace, as the only daughter, felt that her proper place was at home looking after her. According to one of her nieces, in later life Grace rarely mentioned her time in Japan but she did recount experiencing a terrible earthquake at the turn of the century, an event that may well have influenced her decision to resign. She was a much more private person than Hannah and perhaps she simply became disenchanted with all the wranglings that had taken place. No evidence exists to suggest Grace fell out with Hannah; indeed, despite their vastly different person-alities, they seem to have worked together in exceptional harmony.

Meanwhile, in the CMS corridors of power, the debate surrounding the Kyushu controversy continued at an agonisingly slow pace. The meeting following the February one did not take place until 19 June, when, having examined the evidence against Hannah, the parent committee decided that it was not sufficient to require an answer from her. However, if the committee judged that Hannah was being unfairly treated, the members were nevertheless pragmatic enough to realise that it would be not be desirable to send her back to Kumamoto.

During the next month Hannah put in writing her own case to the committee. Normally Hannah was an articulate woman but on this occasion it seems she was over zealous. Until now, the committee had adopted a relatively neutral position but having read Hannah's letters on the subject, the members changed their minds. Not only did they now require from her a formal answer to the accusations put before them but, in a strengthening of their previous position, they actually recommended that Hannah should not under any circumstances be allowed to return to Kumamoto.

Hannah had lost. To be fair, it was the duty of the committee to consider the well-being of the Kyushu mission as a whole. Whatever the rights and wrongs of the situation, the practical solution to the problem was simply to remove the member of the team who appeared to be causing all the trouble. But if the parent committee now thought it had the situation under control, it underestimated both Hannah's determination and her commitment to the Kaishun Hospital.

Once she realised that there was no possibility of her being allowed to return to Kumamoto while working for the CMS, Hannah seized the initiative and offered her resignation. At the same time she made clear her intention to return to Kumamoto even if it meant going independently. On 5 December 1900 Baring-Gould (for the first time not addressing her as "<u>My</u> dear Miss Riddell") wrote to her, formally accepting her resignation and summing up his letter with the following: "Earnestly do we trust that abundant spiritual blessing will rest upon your future work for Christ, though you will not be astonished at my adding that, in the interest of the cause of God, we regret that at the present time, and under the special circumstances you should resume residence in Kumamoto."

Indeed, the committee had urged Hannah to remain in England until the return of both Brandram and Hutchinson (then imminent), when there would have been an opportunity to discuss in the open the whole unhappy situation. But Hannah, knowing of Grace's intentions to resign, must have been more anxious than ever to return as soon as possible to Kumamoto, realising that without her presence, the entire project would fail. Before she left, however, the committee warned her in no uncertain terms that if she did not behave with extreme tact and wisdom, serious difficulties would befall the Kumamoto church. At that stage, however, none of the parties involved could have foreseen the events which, within a month of Hannah's resignation, tragically resolved the issue between her and Brandram.

The state of Brandram's health had been a worry for some time. Since October he had barely slept and at a missionary conference he attended in Tokyo he had appeared strained and tired. But as he and his family were about to leave for their furlough in England there had not been too much concern. Back in Kumamoto, he had been unable to sleep at all and on 22 December he had broken down completely, becoming extremely violent and smashing everything he could lay his hands on.

Guarded by a fellow missionary and four Japanese, he was taken overnight by train to Nagasaki. There, having removed all the furniture, they kept him in the bishop's chapel. The local doctor refused to admit Brandram into his hospital but recommended he be taken to Hong Kong, where there was a good asylum, though he feared that no effective treatment existed for him. A German boat refused to carry him but a Japanese ship offered him passage, if a suitable escort could be provided. Somehow, on the evening of 29 December, Fuller and Hind managed to get Brandram aboard the *Nippon maru,* where the doctor gave him drugs to control his violence. The next morning he seemed slightly better but soon fell into a coma and in the afternoon died of exhaustion and heart failure. When the ship reached Woosung the next day, Brandram's coffin, covered with a Union Jack, was taken by steam launch to Shanghai, where he was buried.

Throughout this sad drama, Mrs. Brandram had been left in Nagasaki, while her four boys were cared for by Grace Nott in Kumamoto. It was quickly arranged that Grace would accompany the bereaved family back to England as soon as possible. Presumably Grace had intended to await Hannah's return before leaving Japan for good. Whether or not she achieved this is unrecorded but one thing is clear: when Hannah reached Kumamoto, probably in January 1901, she was entering a new phase of her life. Her old antagonist, John Brandram, was dead, Ada had gone far away to Maebashi to work for the Americans, and her chief ally, Grace Nott, was returning to England. She did however, have her faithful Japanese friends, a growing network of supporters back in England, and, above all, the Kaishun Hospital and her beloved patients.

CHAPTER 19

Going Solo

Any relief Hannah felt at being rid of the CMS straitjacket was certainly countered by her pressing financial needs. Although the society had made no direct contribution to the hospital, it had housed her, paid her a salary, and looked after her medical expenses. All these costs she now had to pay herself and Hannah was not by nature a frugal lady.

Money worries notwithstanding, on her return to Kumamoto Hannah moved from Choanji-cho to a fine house on the banks of the Shiraka-wa—436 Furushinyashiki. This was a good residential area, and her neighbours were mostly officers and well-to-do merchants. The house was destroyed in an air raid but photographs show that it was large, comfortable, and set in a fine garden. The Anglican church was round the corner under the care of a Japanese pastor, the Reverend K. Nakamu-ra, and the hospital a twenty-minute jinrikisha ride away. Across the river was a large commercial district and in the distance could be seen the walls of the castle, though the castle itself had been destroyed in the Satsuma Rebellion of 1877. Hannah's house had an agreeable view over the Shirakawa, which although not navigable for steamers was always busy with small boats carrying produce from the countryside.

Having made the difficult decision to resign from the CMS, Hannah set up a formal society of supporters of the hospital with president, patrons, vice-presidents, and council. Although she had spent only a few months in Liverpool, it was to her friends and contacts there that she now

turned for patronage and help. Edward Cropper became her first president and his youngest daughter, Evelyn, although only twenty, made the
bold decision to travel out to Kumamoto and work as Hannah's assistant.

Whatever the difficulties in keeping the hospital running, its excellent
reputation soon spread among the lepers and by 1901 Hannah was
anxious to expand its operations. The Hosokawa family came to her aid
by granting her some three acres of adjoining land (on a 999-year lease)
on which additional accommodation for the patients was quickly built.

Despite such generosity from her friends and well-wishers, both abroad
and in Japan, Hannah found it a struggle to make ends meet during the
two years following her return to Kumamoto. A woman of less courage
and conviction might well have packed her bags and made for home but
Hannah's determination to keep her hospital running at all costs was
such that she was even prepared to eat humble pie before the CMS. On
18 October 1902, the day after her forty-seventh birthday, she wrote a
letter to the Reverend Henry Fox. Her message was twofold: she wanted
the CMS to take on responsibility for the hospital and she wished to
rejoin the society's ranks.

The first part of her letter was a straightforward proposition. The
hospital was prospering. The number of admissions was steadily increasing, and there were two dispensaries for out-patients. Now that it was
legally possible for foreigners to hold a lease on property in Japan for 999
years, the trustees of the hospital had transferred the land and buildings
(worth some three hundred pounds) to Hannah's name. But she was
worried that if anything happened to her, the whole endeavour would
collapse.

> That all may not be lost and the work, if it be God's will perpetuat-
> ed, I must seek its continuity in some form, and as the work of the
> Hospital was commenced under the auspices of the CMS inasmuch
> as I was one of its workers and it lent its powerful support to it, in the
> way of approval and countenance, though not directly financially, it
> is but right to ask the CMS if it will now accept the land and
> buildings and responsibilities as they are.

Hannah must have thought long and hard before she penned her next
request:

The second subject of my letter is more difficult. I wish most respectfully to offer my own services once more to the CMS and to do so unconditionally for service, anywhere in Japan, or any other country.

When with so much pain I felt obliged to sever my connection with the CMS two years ago, it was as those nearest me fully understood not because of any opposition to the CMS but because it seemed to me that my character as a Christian missionary had been so seriously assailed that I could not do any good work anywhere in Japan for God and the CMS if I were moved from Kumamoto. At the same time it was clear that the CMS could not send me back to Kumamoto and so it seemed to my friends and myself I must come <u>alone</u> and take up a very heavy cross here . . . Lest it should appear that for some reason I wish to give up responsibility or to leave Kumamoto I can but say that in the manner of the Hospital I feel like the poor Mother who gave up possession of her child, rather than it should be slain—and as to Kumamoto, it is to me the happiest spot upon earth. Nowhere I think could I find so much earthly happiness and if I have a desire it is to spend my life here with these dear people and the Leper Hospital and its interests.

This was a major climb down. Perhaps even the indomitable Hannah was finding the cross she had chosen too heavy to bear, but it is more likely that she had simply run out of funds and that her plea to Fox was motivated by financial desperation. She may also have been lonely and perhaps judged that the two years which had elapsed since her resignation was enough time for the bitterness felt by her missionary colleagues in the aftermath of Brandram's death to have faded. But Hannah was wrong.

The letter included a postscript which can surely have fooled no one:

P.S. Perhaps I should explain that I have not as yet mentioned this letter to the Bishop in Kiushu, lest it should seem that I was endeavouring to turn opinion towards Kiushiu and Kumamoto. Whatever the decisions may be, they will be of greater value to me while I can feel that I have not tried to balance them in any way but left it all entirely in God's hands.

In fact, "balancing the decisions" was exactly what Hannah was trying to do. The Bishop of Kyushu was still her arch-enemy Henry Evington, and she knew full well that he would do his best to frustrate both her plans for the hospital and her reinstatement into the CMS. Using her old technique, she tried to go over Evington's head and persuade the authorities in London directly with her own brand of persuasive eloquence.

CMS reaction to Hannah's proposals was predictable and neatly summed up in an internal memo dated 10 December 1902:

> I fail to see that the two points raised by Miss R. hang together. The continuity of her Hospital work could be easily secured by the action taken by Miss C. Newton of Jaffa, who though not a CMS missionary, has secured the ultimate reversion of the Hospital to us, though it remains hers for her lifetime. Miss R. would be wise to take this course.
>
> As to her return to us as a Missionary, the way seems fraught with difficulties. It would be practically impossible to accept her and remove her from Kiushiu, as the Hospital is so linked with her personally: it would be—I judge—entirely impossible to re-instate her in Kiu Shiu as our Missionary in view of the feeling of the brethren there. Personally, though I think she was in some respects misjudged and hardly treated,
>
> I should deeply deprecate Miss R.'s return to our staff.
>
> Could we not (a) advise her to take the same step as Miss C. Newton did to ensure continuity of her work, and (b) advise her to retain the Police work and not re-open the question of CMS? If she does re-open it, I think it should only be through the <u>local authorities</u>.

Sometime in January 1903 Hannah received a reply from Baring-Gould telling her that her proposals had been forwarded to the Kyushu missionaries who would consider both issues before any decisions were made. At that point Hannah either realised there was no hope of her old antagonists welcoming her back into the fold, or some other event occurred (possibly an unexpected boost to the hospital's finances) which caused her to change her mind. While expressing enthusiasm at the suggestion of the hospital reverting to the CMS on her death, she wrote back that regretfully circumstances had arisen that obliged her to defer her offer of personal service to the society.

This news was no doubt greeted with sighs of relief by both the parent committee in London and the missionaries in Kyushu. There remained outstanding, however, the issue of the hospital's future, a matter that was finally debated in March 1903 by the Kyushu conference, made up of the same old cast of characters—Hannah's embittered detractors. Unsurprisingly, they unanimously turned down the proposal for the hospital. In the minutes of the meeting, it was pointed out that the running costs of the hospital amounted to six hundred pounds per year and that there was little hope of raising an adequate endowment fund. Also noted was the fact that the offer had not come from the hospital council. Evington had made enquiries behind the scenes and discovered that Hannah had not even told Evelyn Cropper of her intentions. As her father was president of the council and Evelyn herself a member, Hannah's approach struck Evington as strange. Hannah's methods were often unorthodox, perhaps on this occasion even bordering on the unethical, but his relish in wrong-footing her indicates that nothing had changed his deep hostility to her. Nor had anything happened to alter the missionaries' view concerning the long-term value of the hospital, as the minutes of the meeting make obvious:

> This Conference would further point out that the work of the Hospital would occupy an undue portion of the time of the European Missionary staff of the Kumamoto Station and is of opinion that in proportion to the expenditure of time and money entailed the results are likely to be far less than with ordinary work.
>
> In accordance with the above consideration (whilst heartily sympathising with the object of the work) the Conference cannot recommend the Society to make any change in its present relations to the Hospital.

The missionaries could not have expressed their view more clearly. Compared with the "ordinary work" of preaching, teaching, praying, and proselytising, caring for a few lepers was a waste of funds and human resources. From today's perspective, this attitude towards the leper hospital is extraordinary. But given that the missionaries' outward measure of success was the number of conversions achieved, they were feeling pressure, as results in recent years had been disappointing:

> The power of Buddhism is great, and the power of Shintoism; and the power of Agnosticism; and, above all, the power of self and sin. Although baptisms in Japan are numerous . . . the total number of Christians has not increased latterly, owing to the very large leakage through backsliding and apostasy.[1]

Only a few months before the March meeting, a report had been sent to London implying the acquisition of 431 souls, a number which embarrassingly then had to be retracted when only four were baptised.[2]

Even had there been no clash of personalities, it is doubtful that the mission's view of the hospital would have been markedly different. Mesmerised by the problem of getting their message across to the vast numbers of unconverted souls surrounding them, the missionaries considered the hospital an unproductive distraction. The outcome of Hannah's latest bout with the CMS proved to be final and unequivocal. If she wanted the hospital to continue, she would have to rely solely on her own resources and abilities.

CHAPTER 20

The Policeman's Friend

Despite these worries and the ever-present demands of the hospital, during this period Hannah was able to take up another project which obviously gave her great satisfaction. In 1902 she became editor of a periodical called *The Policeman and Warders' Friend*, a monthly religious and educational magazine designed to stimulate and nurture interest in Christianity among the Japanese police.

The samurai had been Japan's ruling class for over seven hundred years. When they lost their formal status in the early 1870s a significant number of them joined the fledgling police force, which was to become a powerful and authoritarian organisation, one which had obvious appeal to disaffected (and often impoverished) samurai.

Hannah's first contact with the police came about as a result of a burglary in 1898. The night after Grace Nott returned from her long furlough in England, a thief broke into the house and stole money which had been put aside to settle the hospital accounts. But the outcome of this catastrophe was not all grief. Hannah, never one to miss a good evangelistic opportunity, became friendly with the Kumamoto chief of police, who before long was asking her to give both him and his officers English lessons.

The previous year in Osaka a CMS lady missionary had started a school for the police, teaching young men English and the Bible. Her efforts had been so well received that another school soon opened in Tokyo at the request of the police authorities themselves. The success of the CMS female missionaries' work among young Japanese men clearly surprised the society, which noted "in most Mission-fields any such influence is neither possible nor desirable; but Japan is exceptional, as it is in so many other respects."[1]

For many Japanese men, the idea of women working and teaching independently was still a novelty, a view that may account for some of the ladies' success in penetrating such unexpected corners of Japanese society as the police force.

Certainly Hannah always seemed to have been more at ease working with men than with members of her own sex, a cause of further CMS displeasure since it was strongly felt that missionary work among the women in Kumamoto had been badly neglected during her tenure. Hannah's childhood had occurred against a military back-drop and her mother's first husband, Samuel, had himself been a policeman at the time of his death. Police work appealed to Hannah and she threw herself into it with her usual energy and enthusiasm.

The International Christian Police Association had its headquarters in Kumamoto, and Hannah was appointed (or self-appointed) to edit *The Policeman and Warders' Friend*. The publication is a delightful period piece and an excellent example of the mingling of cultures at grass-roots level that was arguably the missionaries' most lasting contribution to Meiji Japan. The few copies of the magazine that survive (discovered in a second-hand bookshop by members of the Japanese Correctional Association) present Hannah in full flow, clearly enjoying the rewards of editorship.

The magazine had a circulation throughout Japan of about fourteen hundred[2] and it set out to combine English instruction with topical articles heavily laced with Christian ideology. Hannah wrote editorials with such titles as "Your Sons," "Apple Blossom," and "Some New Year Thoughts." Other regular contributors included Grace Nott (writing from England), Evelyn Cropper, the Japanese pastor K. Nakamura, and even Bishop Evington, who during the Russo-Japanese War contributed a monthly column entitled "Prayers for the Soldiers in the Field and Their Families at Home." The menu was varied from "Nursery Hints" (in the "Wives Corner") to "Faith and Salvation," "Scientists and Religion," and "Abraham Lincoln's Faith." The evils of alcohol was a recurrent theme and there were articles such as "Temperance—a Short History of

Japanese Sake," "The Dangerous Nature of Beer," and "How a Wife Converted Her Husband to Temperance."

Readers were invited to write a monthly essay on such subjects as the visit of the Prince of Connaught, Russian prisoners, the San Francisco earthquake, home-coming soldiers, and the new Anglo-Japanese alliance. The magazine advised those who wished to have their work "corrected, and advice or instruction given about making out the same, may do so by sending it to Miss Riddell at 436 Furushinyashiki."

The policemen were also given the opportunity to practice their translation skills. Some of the pieces offered for this purpose were meant to be humorous:

> "I think you need not learn English at all," said an old man to his son, who was poring over his English Reader.
> "Why?" asked the son in astonishment.
> "Well," replied the father, "this afternoon I went to a church to hear an Englishman preach. I understood every word he said, although I have never taken any English lessons."
> At this the young man was naturally very much astonished, but afterwards found that the Englishman had spoken in Japanese!

Other items, such as this exercise in the comparative, were unashamedly patriotic:

> The Russians are brave but the Japanese are braver.
> Japan has become one of the greatest nations of the world.
> Russia has found Japan mightier than she expected.
> The future may have severer defeats in store for Russia.
> Better soldiers than the Japanese are hard to find.

This last exercise appeared in the May edition of 1905, when Japan had been at war with Russia for over a year. Since the turn of the century tension had been building up between the two countries over their competing territorial ambitions in the region, but the immediate cause of the war was the Russian occupation of Manchuria. British sentiment was firmly behind the Japanese. As G. H. Moule, stationed at the time in Kumamoto, put it in *The Spirit of Japan*, "Never before had a comparatively small Asiatic nation confronted, by itself, one of the greatest military powers in Europe. The stupendous nature of this conflict with the Colossus of the North and the tremendous importance of the issues at stake made the spectacle of national heroism more than usually impressive."

As had been the case with the war against China ten years earlier, Hannah and the other foreigners living in Kumamoto were well placed to witness the conduct of the Japanese soldiers since the city was still the headquarters of the Sixth Division and once more a hive of military activity. The missionaries were impressed with what they saw:

> I saw the reservists coming in from the country and bidding a cheerful farewell to their relations and friends. I watched these men billeted in the town, helping in the house-work, nursing and amusing children . . . As I remember, I never met a drunken or disorderly soldier. Shortly after, the Sixth Division was ordered to the front. Day and night the troop-trains were despatched, and for long hours at a stretch men, women, and children waited to send the soldiers off with waving flags and loud shouts of <u>banzai</u>! One wondered which to admire more, the cheerful, manly bearing of the soldiers, or the patient enthusiasm of the waiting crowds—an enthusiasm which hid many an aching heart and suppressed many a tear.[3]

The Russo-Japanese War offered further opportunities for Hannah to publish her views on life. On 8 July 1905 the *Japan Weekly Mail* printed a letter from a Japanese military doctor, forwarded to them by Hannah, in which he expressed his concern for the spiritual welfare of the wounded soldiers lying in hospital in Manchuria:

> Spiritual felicity is a thing one naturally longs for even under the best of conditions. Is it to be wondered at then that these poor soldiers, who are confined in hospitals in a strange land, so far away from their dear ones, should yearn for something more than drugs or food? In fact those men become peculiarly thoughtful and keenly susceptible to religious and moral influences, and many of them seem as if their whole souls had been suddenly awakened by their recent baptism of fire . . . Newspapers, magazines, phonographs, etc., all fill their own place, but still there is a gap which we propose to fill by publishing two magazines of about 200 pages each, one of which is to be called "Consolation for the Sick and Wounded."

The doctor appealed to the foreign community for contributions, and Hannah was quick to oblige him. In her essay on imperialism she expounded her beliefs on such weighty subjects as the benefits of English colonial policy, duty, trade policy, and the brotherhood of man—not a light read.[4]

While Japanese soldiers were struggling with Hannah's global view, Western observers were being stirred by the spectacle of Japanese chivalry concerning the treatment of their Russian prisoners. Their reports are an extraordinary contrast to accounts of Japanese treatment of prisoners a mere thirty years later:

> Many Russian prisoners are stationed on the island and I was tremendously interested in the good time they were having. The Japanese officials are entertaining them violently with concerts, picnics, etc.
>
> Of course it is practically impossible for the men to escape but I don't believe they want to. A cook has actually been brought from Vladivostock so that they may have Russian food, and the best things in the markets are sent to them. The prisoners I saw seemed in high spirits, and were having as much fun as a lot of school boys out on a lark. I don't wonder! It is lots more comfortable being a prisoner in Japan than a soldier in Manchuria.[5]

Hannah admired the heroic deeds of the Japanese as much as anyone but the war was causing her grave problems. As she wrote in her hospital report covering the years 1903–5, the sympathies of both Japanese and English friends had been given almost exclusively to the wounded soldiers and their families, with the consequence that funds for the hospital had been severely "distressed."

There was, however, some good news. The much needed mortuary, isolation ward, and quiet room for the dying had been provided by friends in Kobe. More prosaic but essential improvements to the hospital were the enlarged storeroom for winter bedding and a new bathroom for the nurses and attendants. Hannah was proud to note that nearly all the forty-two patients had been baptised and some of them had established a branch of the Christian Endeavour Society. Her report for 1903–5 quoted one patient who had said, "We cannot hope to be beautiful to look at, but we can try to lead beautiful lives."

CHAPTER 21

The Big Time

The first detailed hospital accounts (or at least those that have survived) are from 1903 and 1904. Those accounts note that forty percent of the running costs were provided by English subscribers, the great majority of them women. The rest was raised in Japan by both Japanese and expatriates. Lady MacDonald, wife of the British Ambassador, was listed as a patroness and Count Shigenobu Okuma and Dr. Erwin Baelz as patrons. The latter was a distinguished German doctor working in Tokyo, who attended many leading figures of the time, both foreign and Japanese, including the Emperor himself. Baelz's name, together with that of Dr. Iwai of the Red Cross Hospital and two professors of medicine from the Imperial University in Tokyo, added considerable weight to the medical credentials of the Kaishun Hospital.

An even more illustrious name was that of Count Okuma, statesman and founder of Waseda University, whose connection with the hospital was a major public-relations coup for Hannah. Exactly how Hannah came to know Okuma, one of the best-known political figures of Meiji Japan, is a mystery but his hometown, Saga, is not far from Kumamoto and possibly she wrote to him enlisting his support for the hospital merely. on the grounds that he was a celebrated son of Kyushu. Their association went back at least as far as 1901, when, at the time of the hospital's expansion, Okuma had donated a number of cherry and maple trees.

Regarded as something of a radical by his oligarchical colleagues,

Okuma was a strong supporter of constitutional government and of Britain, despite a fiery confrontation he had early in his career with the British Minister, the formidable Sir Harry Parkes, over the issue of the persecution of Christians. Okuma had fiercely defended the Japanese government's position to do what it liked outside the treaty ports.

By the time Okuma became a patron of the Kaishun Hospital, he had served the government as Finance Minister, as Foreign Minister, and for a few months in 1898 as Prime Minister. Even his critics admired Okuma's courage. In 1889, when he was negotiating revision of the treaties, an extremist, in an act of desperation, to rescue (as he perceived it) Japan's national honour, threw a bomb at Okuma's carriage. Although Okuma lost a leg as a result of the attack, he so admired his assailant (who committed suicide on the spot) for his willingness to die for his principles that he always sent money to the man's family on the anniversary of the assassination attempt. Okuma knew everyone of any consequence in Japan, and his support was to prove vital to Hannah's cause.

But of even greater significance was the commitment of another outstanding Meiji figure—Viscount Eiichi Shibusawa, a protégé of Okuma's. Shibusawa is often described as the founder of Japanese banking but is remembered today almost as much for his philanthropy. In the course of his long life he was involved with hundreds of charitable organisations and causes, both big and small. As president of the Tokyo City Poor House, Shibusawa regularly came across lepers who had been brought in off the streets, an experience which revived memories of his own childhood:

> There lived a family very close to our house. I had a friend in that family, a boy one year younger than me. His mother was a leper and none of the villagers would approach her. But my mother, who was exceedingly humane, continued her intercourse with the suffering woman. Influenced by my mother, I played with the boy not infrequently, but with a mixed feeling of hatred and pity. In the meantime, the boy's mother was shut in, hardly ever to be seen by her neighbors, and it was rumoured that the boy too was to be confined at home. When I heard this, my heart was filled with sorrow and compassion.[1]

Surprisingly Hannah did not secure Shibusawa as a patron of the hospital, but in her efforts to interest him in her work, she was pushing at an open door, as he himself made plain:

> By unappointed and spontaneous contacts with some of them [lepers], I came to learn their mental condition, in which was disclosed their attitude of revolt and cursing towards the community wherein they lived. They entertained desperate destructive ideas against the general public. I found painful reasons why they could not be in a wholesale manner dismissed as social outcasts when I heard the story of their experiences. Hence . . . a reason why something must be done from the standpoint of social welfare took hold of me.[2]

Soon after the Russo-Japanese War, Shibusawa went to America with a group of Japanese businessmen. Elated by Japan's new international status in the wake of her unexpected victory over Russia, the delegation was surprised to find foreigners who were still unprepared to accept that Japan was a country of "honour and culture" on the grounds that while she claimed to have risen to the front rank of nations, she was yet incapable of controlling the dreaded disease of leprosy.[3]

An embarrassing incident that is alleged to have taken place in front of the British Embassy may also have helped to focus Japanese authorities' attention on the problem. A dying leper outside the gates of the embassy was brought to the notice of the ambassador, Sir Claude MacDonald, who remarked that it was a shame for a top-ranking nation like Japan to have lepers. The missionaries may have had problems getting across to the Japanese the notion of "sin" but everyone knew the meaning of "shame." The ambassador's words stung.

The MacDonalds had previously served in Peking, where in 1900 Sir Claude had won distinction commanding the foreign legations' tiny defence force during the eight-week Boxer siege. Lady MacDonald had tirelessly tended the sick and wounded throughout the conflict and was afterwards rewarded with the Royal Red Cross. The MacDonalds later enjoyed the rare experience of reading their own obituaries, as it was assumed back in England that they had been killed. In fact, they were very much alive and from China went on to spend twelve years in Japan. During this time Sir Claude presided over three Anglo-Japanese agreements and in 1905, in recognition of the two countries' strengthening relations, the British legation was upgraded to an embassy.

Lady MacDonald was an attractive and witty woman and all her life deeply involved in charity work. Although during the Boxer crisis she was noted for keeping the missionaries at arm's length (the *Times'* correspondent complained that no missionary was invited to dine at the minister's house during the siege), she became one of Hannah's most stalwart supporters and continued to send money to the hospital long after she and her husband returned to England in 1912.

Money, in 1905, was Hannah's overriding preoccupation. Just how dire the hospital's financial condition had become is made clear in a letter Hannah wrote to Count Okuma on 15 October:

Dear Count Okuma,

Please allow me to thank you for your most kind reception yesterday. After leaving you I went to Viscount Okubo's and though we talked a great deal about the Endowment Fund I wish to create for the Hospital, I did not ask them for any money. Do you think they would give if I did so? Marquis and Marchioness Hosokawa received me most kindly and so did Mr. Mitsui to whom I gave your kind message. Mrs. Hirooka was there but she had visitors and I could not see her.

When I reached home I found a letter from the Hong Kong and Shanghai Bank which though quite a kind letter distracts me very much. The Bank has allowed me to overdraw to the amount of 1,500 yen and it wrote asking me to attend to the matter at once. The Bank has been most kind and even in this letter advised me with regard to the endowment fund I wished to create, suggesting that all the money for the Endowment should be placed in Government Bonds at 6%.

I am sorry to give you so much trouble but I do not in the least know what to do about the Bank and how to meet the rest of the claims for this year. October, November and December will together require another 1,500 yen reaching a total of 3,000 yen!! Do you think anyone would lend that sum now until the end of January? I am writing to England begging for money and perhaps some would give here and Lady MacDonald intends to do something in January to help the Hospital.

If I could put 3,000 yen in the bank now, I could pay the lender as the money came in. But it is difficult to pay the monthly wages and kayoi [living-out maids] in that way and the bank! They have to be met.

I cannot suppose anyone would give 3,000 yen to help the present distress, but perhaps someone, if I only knew wealthy people, might lend it, with small interest to the end of January. If you would be so good as to give me your valuable advice, I should be most grateful for I am indeed very anxious.

Lack of money was a familiar problem to Hannah, and her present situation must have brought back all too vividly the nightmare of her bankruptcy in Wales sixteen years earlier. This time, however, she was more fortunate—deliverance was at hand.

On 6 November, Okuma and Shibusawa set up a meeting at the Bankers' Club in Tokyo with the aim of debating the leprosy issue in Japan. Hannah was invited to address a powerful gathering of some twenty-five men from government, business, and journalism on the topic of "What Should We Do for the Lepers in Japan?" The sight of this statuesque Englishwoman speaking with such passion and sincerity on a subject that had traditionally been ignored by their fellow countrymen clearly stirred those present. Hannah's claim that if only Japan were to spend the cost of one destroyer on alleviating leprosy, the problem would be solved, was wildly optimistic. But Hannah knew how to work a crowd, and her words were so effective that they are said to have inspired Shizutaro Kubota, head of the Home Office Board of Health, to recognise the urgent need of legislation for the care of lepers. Kubota's reaction to Hannah's eloquence was significant. A year earlier, when Shibusawa had proposed building a special leprosy hospital in Tokyo, Kubota had violently opposed the idea, blaming Shibusawa for wanting to bring all the lepers of Japan to Tokyo, an all too familiar "not in my backyard" reaction.

The Bankers' Club conference was not only an important landmark in Japan's fight against leprosy but also a vital turning point in Hannah's own life. Until that occasion, she had been a worthy missionary struggling to keep afloat a provincial project. Now, suddenly, she found herself in a leading role centre stage, playing to an influential audience eager to hear her words and act on her advice.

After this pivotal meeting, events flowed with some speed. A committee was quickly formed to deal with the issues that had arisen and following its first deliberations, on 9 December, Okuma was able to report to Hannah that it had agreed on a number of important measures: the government would submit a leprosy-prevention bill to the Diet; efforts would be made to educate the public about leprosy; government funds would be made available for research into the disease; and people of influence would be mobilised to give financial assistance to the Kaishun Hospital. Okuma was a man of his word. A week after the committee met at his house, the Kumamoto Prefectural Assembly wrote Hannah a flattering letter, praising her work and offering 1,500 yen to the hospital.

At about the same time, in 1906, another important development in the history of the Kaishun Hospital occurred when it became a "juridical person." This change meant that instead of being registered personally under Hannah's name the hospital now received a charter as a non-profit-making foundation and was thus exempt from taxation. Achieving this status in Meiji Japan was not easy, and this case was probably another example of Okuma's influence working in Hannah's favour.

On 16 January 1906, exactly fifteen years after she first arrived in Japan, Hannah received the ultimate seal of official approval, the Medal of the Blue Ribbon. Her policy of going straight to the top had paid off handsomely. Not only had her work been recognised by the Japanese government but her views on the treatment of leprosy were being sought by people at the highest level of public life in Japan.

CHAPTER 22

Theories

It is not surprising that after ten years of working with lepers, Hannah had formed strong opinions concerning their treatment, not all of them correct. Although as early as 1874 Hansen had proved that leprosy was caused by a bacterium, Hannah insisted that the disease was hereditary and remained convinced all her life that sex segregation was the only way to eradicate it, as the following passages from a 1930 issue of the *Japan Christian Quarterly* make clear:

> Despite the many attempts in many countries to cure, by medicine and by prayer, no absolutely authenticated cure has taken place since the days of Our Lord.
>
> But why not? His Power is still the same. Sometimes I wonder if it is withheld to compel the nations to take the one plain way open to rid the world of this awful terror: it has been proved that there is one way namely, sex-segregation. There should be <u>no leper children</u> . . . An experience of several generations leads us to definitely decide that the disease is both hereditary and contagious but not infectious.

This last sentence expresses muddled thinking. There is no difference between infection and contagion, and a disease that is hereditary cannot at the same time be infectious. But Hannah had a theory, one she was not

prepared to give up easily, even in the face of scientific evidence. The closest she ever came to admitting there was another side to the argument was in the following passage from a report she wrote in 1925:

> The much discussed question as to whether leprosy is hereditary or infectious remains unsolved, but in Japan (whatever it may be in any other countries) one is almost obliged to believe that it is hereditary rather than infectious, except by inoculation. There is however a growing tendency among Japanese medical men to call it a "family predisposition" rather than use the word hereditary, which brands a family and spells its ruin.

Having decided that a policy of strict sex segregation was the only answer to the problem, Hannah developed clear views on how it should be implemented. In 1914 she set out her ideas in a letter to Count Okuma, who was by then, for the second time, Prime Minister:

> What I should like to suggest is that . . . two portions of land should be appropriated in each Ken [prefecture] as far apart as possible, and that all the leper men of that Ken should be very comfortably housed and cared for in one place, and the women in the other . . . Another great difficulty is the children of leper patients: and for them special regulations would be necessary. They should of course be allowed every possible chance in life . . . but I think they should not be allowed to marry for two generations, and although that seems a very stringent thing, I believe their patriotism could be appealed to, and boys and girls would grow up with the idea that marriage was not for them, though every other joy and comfort in life might be theirs.

It was true that children born to lepers ran a high risk of catching the disease, and there was the problem of caring for the children when their parents could not or had died. Nevertheless, to deny the comfort of marriage to people who were already deprived of so much in life was an unnecessarily hard measure in view of the existence of birth-control.

Although Hannah enjoyed the company of men, especially when she was teaching them, it is difficult not to gain the impression that the whole subject of procreation was abhorrent to her. She was a determined lady but even she could not abolish original sin. However, she could justify banishing sex from the Kaishun Hospital and from her hypothetical leper communities on the spurious grounds that total abstinence was the only way to halt the spread of the disease.

In the Kaishun Hospital, described by the patient Keisai Aoki in *Mission to Okinawa* as having an almost monastic atmosphere, it was observed that Hannah even disliked seeing patients feed a pair of birds in the same cage. When her dog was on heat, she would sorrowfully remark, "My doggie is a real prodigal." Marriage was not allowed at the hospital under any circumstances. If a couple fell in love and let their secret be known, they were required to leave the hospital, treatment that conjures up the image of Adam and Eve being expelled from the Garden of Eden. Such was the force of Hannah's personality that, despite the fact the men's and women's wards were separated by only a low hedge, scarcely anyone ever dared cross the barrier.[1] There were, however, plenty of other places for them to meet, and love affairs among the patients were not a rarity.[2]

Towards the end of Hannah's life, the Japanese chaplain to the hospital, a widower, the Reverend Takuya Arato, wished to remarry. Hannah strongly disapproved. Arato was nearly seventy, his bride little more than a girl, and Hannah did her best to dissuade him, even offering to employ an extra servant for him. His marriage nevertheless went ahead and even took place in the hospital chapel. The sting in the tail was a congratulatory speech which centred on the unfortunate story of a woman who was divorced by her husband after only ten days of marriage because she cooked excessive amounts of bean curd. The cold draught of Hannah's disapproval proved too much and the Aratos departed.[3]

There is no question, however, that Keisai Aoki, the author of this anecdote, was anything but a devoted fan of Hannah's, and he was the first to acknowledge that even when patients left the hospital under difficult circumstances, they were never abandoned but continued to receive letters and gifts from Hannah long after their departure. One man who had absconded from the hospital recalled receiving a letter from her a few days later: "My heart was throbbing when I opened the envelope, quite expecting it to contain a scolding from her. I wept bitterly, for there was not one word of reproach, but a one-yen bill fell out and the words 'Please use this for anything you want.'"[4] In those days a bowl of noodles cost eight sen and a hundred sen was equivalent to one yen.

Despite the "monastic" atmosphere of the Kaishun, the great majority of patients considered themselves very lucky to be there. The consensus was that for people who were only lightly afflicted by the disease any sanatorium would suffice, but for those seriously ill, the Kaishun was unquestionably their first choice.

Hannah's insistence on sex segregation may have been unnecessarily dogmatic but she was on very firm ground when advocating the vital need for a leprosarium to have a good water supply and drainage system, clean, comfortable quarters for the patients, and a pleasant, hygienic environment for them to live in. Leprosy was neither hereditary nor was it sexually transmitted but it did flourish in conditions of poverty, squalour, and deprivation.

The much longed-for cure for leprosy was still thirty odd years away but by 1910 the disease had at last been recognised by the Japanese authorities as a genuine problem and they had taken the first steps to deal with it. Hannah was now a celebrated figure whose opinions were valued by some of the most distinguished people in the country. What is more, she was loved and revered by her "children." She had come a long way since her first visit to the Honmyoji temple and could justifiably feel satisfaction with what she had accomplished. However, the ultimate achievement—a cure for leprosy—was as elusive as ever.

As a convinced Christian, Hannah naturally felt that prayer and faith were essential parts of the search for a cure but she did recognise that science also had a role. Regrettably, high morals and fresh air were not enough, however sincerely they were served up. Although Hannah had spent most of her adult life working with the disease, her grasp of its causes and pathology was remarkably weak. But it must be said in her defence that she was not the only one working with leprosy to be confused. Many highly qualified doctors were equally baffled by the disease.

It is to Hannah's credit that, acknowledging the importance of medical research (even if, on occasion, she preferred to ignore its results), she decided to establish a laboratory in the grounds of the hospital. In 1917 Michitaro Uchida was employed as its first director, having been interviewed for the job by Hannah in the lounge at the Imperial Hotel in Tokyo. What she had failed to tell him on that occasion was that the laboratory had not yet been built. When he arrived at the hospital to take up his post, he was surprised to be shown into his "laboratory," a tiny three-mat room with no equipment. However, Hannah did demonstrate to Uchida the seriousness of her purpose by giving him the princely annual salary of 1,000 yen, a contrast to his previous earnings of 250 yen.

During the lean years of the First World War, raising money from England and America was particularly difficult, and Hannah decided to approach the Governor of Osaka, Marquis Toshitaka Okubo, for help to fund the laboratory. Okubo offered his full support, and the money for the venture was somehow found. A year after Uchida became director, the laboratory was completed and described as "a beautiful white building equipped with a drawing-room where Miss Riddell could rest when she came."[5] Uchida was surprised when he first started working at the hospital by the way Hannah moved freely among the patients without wearing a mask, gloves, or any other protective clothing and was perfectly happy to touch them. Impressed by her example, he too soon lost his inhibitions. Uchida had two assistants and a student from the Fifth Higher School, Matsuke Miyazaki, who later became director of the Keifu-en, the local public leprosarium.

A couple was also employed to do the chores around the laboratory. (There was, for example, no flushing lavatory, only a sandbox.) One evening when the electricity failed, the couple put a brazier in the incubator, loyally staying up all night to feed it charcoal, in a desperate but fruitless effort to maintain the temperature and save the doctor's precious bacilli.

Occasionally the laboratory provided a treat for the lepers. Rabbits were used in some of the experiments and after the creatures had delivered up the parts of them required by medical science, their remains were turned into a fine sukiyaki feast for the patients. But Hannah was adamantly against the use of animals in experiments, an attitude that often placed her researchers in an awkward position.

The gentle Dr. Ryoichi Jingu became chief doctor at the hospital in 1926, and part of his research involved the killing of mice. When Hannah heard this, she was appalled, insisting that attempts to culture bacilli should be made only in human blood or milk. Dr. Jingu therefore had to rely on another Christian doctor in Kumamoto, a gynaecologist, to keep him well supplied with milk from his patients.

Over the years a succession of distinguished doctors worked in the Kaishun laboratory and if, despite their dedicated efforts, none of them achieved a major breakthrough, neither at least did they make any false claims of success. Until effective sulfone drugs were finally developed in the 1940s the victims of leprosy were constantly having their hopes raised with promises of wonder cures only to have them dashed when the medicines produced no improvement in their condition or, more often, actually made it worse. Many lepers never even attempted to take medicine, choosing instead to put their trust in Buddha and a variety of other gods to restore their health:

> First I worshipped at the Reizan-ji, then the temples in Tosa and around Iyo, all in all, eighty-eight holy precincts. Finally I received the dedicated creed in the Okubo Temple in Sankui. The tour was really difficult, a distance of some 920 miles on foot beset with all kinds of obstacles and hardships. It involved passing the Yasaka-yahama-no-ken, the steep precipices scowling down on the eight slopes and eight beaches and the valley of the None Mountain where the wolves lived . . . And at Iki-ki-no-Jizo-san I bought one thousand pieces of paper about 1 x 3.3 cm called "one thousand sheets pass," on each of which the words *na-mu-ami-da-butsu* were neatly written in Chinese-style characters. I would swallow one each day before dawn . . . The saying goes that if any deformed person trusts Jizo-san and swallows one thousand of these papers, one a day, he will be healed and his body will be restored to its original healthy state. But when the season of touring on foot had passed and autumn was approaching I could see no evidence of recovery. Moreover it was getting colder day by day. At last both physically and mentally exhausted, weary of this world and overwhelmed with discouragement, I began to long for the day I would die.[6]

The alternative to religion was to experiment with the countless quack medicines on offer, of which the following, described in the *Japan Weekly Mail* on 9 September 1911, is a prime example:

> Last Saturday's issue of the *Hochi* reports the discovery of a new treatment of leprosy by the application of "tetrad toxin," a substance extracted from the poisonous elements of the globe-fish [*fugu*] . . . After Dr. Tahara returned home from Europe some twenty years ago he commenced the study of the poison contained in the

globe-fish. After much labour he succeeded in extracting the poison element from the ovaries of the fish and from this he prepared a pure white tasteless and odourless powder, soluble in water which he named "tetrad toxin." When tested on rabbits it was found that four milligrams of the powder was sufficient to cause death.

The most common treatment for leprosy during the 1920s and 30s was oil extracted from the ripe seeds of the chaulmoogra tree and injected into the patient. As Hannah pointed out in a lecture she delivered to the Kobe Women's Club in 1924, chaulmoogra oil was hardly a new remedy, having been used in ancient times both in Egypt and China. The treatment had been tried extensively at the leper colony in Hawaii, where it had at first appeared to be highly successful. But the improvement turned out to be temporary, and chaulmoogra oil was eventually discredited.

Science was not able to produce an answer to the problem of leprosy until after Hannah's death. Meanwhile, she contented herself and the audiences she frequently addressed with the story of a thirteen-year-old patient in the Kaishun Hospital who was convinced that he would be restored to health by divine intervention. According to the *Japan Weekly Chronicle* of 20 November 1924, after constant prayer, he was miraculously cured "by God himself."

23

Daily Life

On the thorny question of sex segregation, Hannah often crossed swords with Dr. Kensuke Mitsuda, the most famous Japanese doctor associated with leprosy and one whose views on its treatment were paramount until his death in 1964. He took a more liberal position on the issue than Hannah, believing that too strict a policy would turn patients away from the leprosy hospitals. Dr. Mitsuda wanted to put all lepers into government-run hospitals, believing that total segregation from the general public was the only way to wipe out the disease.[1] It was Mitsuda who, together with Shibusawa, was chiefly responsible for pushing forward the leprosy reforms which finally became law in 1907. This bill made provision for the construction of five leprosaria in different parts of Japan, including the one built in 1909 in Kumamoto, the Keifu-en, which still exists.

In order to distinguish the Kaishun from the state leprosaria, which were required to take in all lepers whatever their background, Hannah introduced certain admission rules after 1909. Those accepted had to have had some education and to have previously led respectable lives, even if they could no longer at the time of admission pay their way. Among the patients were university professors, maids, farmers, policemen, Shinto priests, screen makers, and artists. As the Baltimore *Sun* put it in Hannah's obituary, "Most of the victims . . . are drawn now chiefly from among men and women of birth and education, but no money and no one to help. Most of them before coming to the hospital found their sufferings greatly increased by the possibility of having to mingle with the depraved scum of the roadside."

Hannah encouraged her patients to think of her as "Mother" and when she wrote to a leper, she invariably addressed him or her as "My dear Child." The patients seem to have liked this relationship and for many of them, especially those who entered the hospital at a young age, Hannah was the only mother figure they ever knew.

Several years after Hannah's death, a number of patients recorded their personal memories of her. The fact that she not only cared for them as a collective but was deeply concerned with each individual's welfare emerges very clearly from these reminiscences. But their recollections also invoke the unmistakable image of a traditional English nanny: "We were often scolded by Mother . . . Once she came into the patients' room and said smiling, 'Wouldn't you like to see outside?' We didn't understand what she meant . . . Then she said 'Wipe the dirty glass door.'" One patient recalled being told off for doing her washing when she should have been in prayers and another for letting a piece of pickled radish languish in the kitchen sink. A visit to the hospital by British Ambassador Sir Claude MacDonald was preceded by a massive cleaning operation which Hannah followed up with a military-like inspection that would have done credit to her sergeant father.[2]

By the 1920s, Hannah's visits to the hospital were limited to a couple of days a week, and on those days the patients would make very sure that everything was neat and tidy, the veranda polished like a mirror and the garden swept with a bamboo broom. Occasionally she would appear unexpectedly and find basins or other objects lying around on the floors or clothes hanging on the walls. "A blind person will stumble over this," she would remark or be heard to mutter, "Unbecoming. This is most unsightly."[3]

The patients from the Kaishun were always so much better turned out than the patients from other leprosaria in Kumamoto that they were easily identified by the police if they were found wandering in the town without permission. When the authorities confronted Hannah with such misdemeanours, she would deny them categorically, claiming that her patients would never behave in such a manner. She took great interest in their clothes and at Christmas gave everyone a shawl carefully chosen to suit each person. She made sure they all had warm woollen socks in winter and took pleasure in designing special clothing for those with particular needs.

Hannah was often bossy and overbearing, and her insistence on such high standards of orderliness and dress in the hospital sometimes caused the patients to grumble. Most, however, understood that by living in such civilised surroundings and by being well turned out, they were able to acquire a new pride and dignity which many of them had lost as a result of their dreadful disease. And although the Kaishun Hospital may at times have more closely resembled a British boarding-school than a Japanese hospital, its patients nevertheless had plenty of agreeable memories of their life there—of games and music, the gardens they themselves cultivated, and the occasions when Hannah would cheer up a sick patient with a special treat such as ice-cream.

When, in 1897, Hannah appointed Dr. Miyake the resident doctor at the hospital she could not have made a better choice. Doctor Miyake worked at the Kaishun until his death thirty years later, and he emerges as a genuinely heroic and saintly figure. He learned everything he could about his patients and treated each one as a personal friend. Described by one patient as looking like an undistinguished village school master, he had a gentle appearance that was in marked contrast to that of the officials of the state leprosaria, many of whom were former policemen and tended to treat their patients imperiously, as if they were criminals. Most nights Miyake was called from his bed but he never complained, and it was noted, with some astonishment, that he did the housework to help his sick wife. Indeed, his modesty and simple dress often caused visitors to mistake him for a servant.

Miyake served as a buffer between Hannah and the patients and often sorted out problems when there was a breach of the rules. Cooking in the rooms was forbidden but when Miyake, doing his rounds, sniffed the unmistakable smell of sweet potatoes cooking in kettles, he would merely point out that the water was burning.

Christmas was a cheerful time in the hospital, and the following account of Japanese lepers enjoying a traditional English Christmas in distant Kumamoto, some eight thousand miles from Britain, is a peculiarly touching example of cultural contact:

> It was the custom in the Kaishun Hospital to have the Christmas tree in the hall of the chapel. It was beautifully decorated with tiny

bulbs and coloured papers and silver and golden leaves. There were quantities of clothing, scarves, European dolls, and many other things. These would be divided up by lot. Upon receiving a present, some would give a cry of joy, others would sigh because the clothes did not fit or because they needed one thing but got another. Still others laughed hilariously, as men received women's clothing or vice versa. It was a great sight. Then they would have a programme of hymn singing in chorus or solos. Among the soloists were some who sang so beautifully that the audience was touched. Others had the audience rolling with laughter because of their complete lack of any ear for music. It was always a truly happy and merry Christmas.[4]

Christmas celebrates the birth of Christ and the Kaishun Hospital was nothing if not a profoundly Christian institution. While a leper was not required to be Christian before being admitted to the hospital, there was considerable pressure on him or her to become so afterwards and many of them did. Hannah always emphasised the healing of the spirit as well as the body. She comforted one blind lady, the one who had left the radish in the sink, by telling her that even if she could no longer see with her bodily eye, as a Christian, her spiritual eyes would be opened and she would understand the great mercy of God. A high percentage of Kaishun patients took comfort from such words and from the promise, not only of salvation, but of a complete cure in the next world. Those who were less convinced by the Christian faith were generally content to attend daily prayers and other services expected of them by "Mother."

Some patients, however, resisted and despite claims to the contrary, there was clearly strong pressure on everyone to become baptised. One patient, who just died in 1993 at the age of ninety-two, kept a diary in the early 1930s in which he described how irritated he had been at the attempts to move him into a room with a Christian leper who, Hannah hoped, would influence his beliefs.[5]

The church that was finally built and consecrated on 24 June 1924 was a triumph for Hannah. The Great War in Europe had caused further financial crises for her by diverting donors' money to needs nearer home, and it was many years before enough money could be raised to bring this most cherished dream of hers to fruition. Hannah designed the whole building in every detail and in the process proved herself to be a sensitive and intelligent architect. Instead of reproducing a typical Anglican

Church which would have meant little culturally to its Japanese subscribers, she devised a clever compromise between traditional Japanese architecture and Christian needs. The result was highly satisfactory. A characteristically Japanese roof was discreetly christianised with tiny crosses burned into all its prominent tiles. The whole church was surrounded by a three-foot veranda with a ramp leading up to its entrance, thus simplifying access for those in wheelchairs. Another practical consideration led to the space underneath the church being filled with cement to protect it from ravenous white ants, which were constantly trying to eat the hospital into extinction.

The interior of the church was also a successful blend of cultures. Japanese paper screens (*shōji*), natural wood, and tatami mats on the floor were inherently more familiar to a Japanese congregation than stiff wooden pews and gothic tracery, though the church also did contain prayer desks, book racks, and pictures showing the life of Christ on the walls. Little wonder that one Japanese Christian who visited the church soon after its consecration is said to have remarked, "Here for the first time have I entered a church in Japan where my soul could expand and feel the true spirit of worship!"[6]

The patients certainly needed all the solace they could get, both spiritual or worldly. Despite the relative comfort of the Kaishun Hospital the patients' lives were constantly shadowed by pain and depression, as this diarist, writing just before Hannah's death in 1932, makes graphically clear:

21 April. I had a third operation to remove the pus. I hated the sound of the incision.

3 May. My right foot ached very badly.

4 May. Severe headache.

13 May. I had an operation. The pus filled a basin and splashed on the doctor.

23 July. Neuralgia was severe, it lasted until noon.[7]

The last entry was made in the humid heat of a Kyushu summer at the time of year when Hannah and Ada used to regularly leave Kumamoto to spend a couple of months in the cool mountains of Karuizawa, a thousand miles away.

CHAPTER 24

Karuizawa

While Hannah was establishing herself as an authority on the care of lepers, Ada had been living a more conventional and humdrum missionary existence. Her probationary year with the Americans had passed without problems. Indeed, Hannah had been able to write to the CMS with understandable smugness: "It may interest you to know that my niece not only passed her Exam but came out <u>first</u>! The other examinees were men, one Englishman and two Americans." Since leaving Kumamoto, Ada had been posted some distance north of Tokyo, first to Maebashi, then to Kumagaya, to Urawa, and finally to Mito. Her days were spent teaching, studying Japanese, playing the organ, paying calls, and helping the male clergy with a myriad of assorted tasks.

The American missionary sector was north of Tokyo, which meant that Hannah and Ada were a thousand miles apart for most of the year, until 1923, when Ada returned to work full time in the hospital. When they were separated, the two met as often as they could, and although money was tight, lack of it never seems to have deterred them from taking their annual summer holiday in the mountains.

Their favourite resort was Karuizawa, where, along with hundreds of other missionaries from all over Japan and even from China, they spent the hot sticky months of July and August in comparative comfort. Some of Hannah's critics viewed this seasonal exodus as the expensive habit of a rich lady, but Hannah always claimed that she did not go to Karuizawa to be cool and comfortable but to extract contributions for the hospital from the wealthy foreigners and Japanese who assembled there. On similar grounds, she defended her habit of dressing extravagantly and of staying in style at the Imperial Hotel in Tokyo by maintaining that if she lodged at a cheap address or appeared down-at-heel, no one of influence would be interested in her or the hospital. This explanation was undoubtedly true, but it is also a fact that Hannah enjoyed living well. She was prepared to work long and hard for the betterment of mankind but not to wear a hair shirt while doing so.

Certainly there was little evidence of hardship at the annual gathering of missionaries at Karuizawa, a point bitterly noted in an article in *The Eastern World* dated 28 July 1900:

> The chosen of the Lord have again left the sinful settlements and sweltering plains to take their two months' annual holiday at Karuizawa to praise the Lord who annually helps them to get there, whilst the children of wrath have to slave at their desks eight, nine, yea on maildays, even thirteen and fourteen hours . . . Where, further, is it recorded that Christ and his Apostles took annual holidays? What Japan wants are not men and women to point out to the people some particularly short route to heaven, but men and women who have done years of honest hard work in some useful trade and who can and will teach others to do the same. Let the missionaries, therefore, instead of mumbling prayers and chanting hymns at summer resorts, teach a couple of thousand young men and young women type-setting, printing, bookbinding, machine ruling, envelope-making, engraving in wood, copper, and steel, electroplating, joiners' and carpenters' work.

The missionaries, not unnaturally, took a rather different view of their summer holidays:

> The work of the missionary is most trying, and the demands on his health and strength are very exhausting. The petty worries and trials that constantly meet him, the rivalries and quarrels which his converts bring to him for settlement, the care of the churches, anxiety about his family, etc., are a constant strain on his vital force, in order to withstand which it is necessary that he should have

regular periods of rest and recreation . . . It is customary in Japan for missionaries to leave their fields of work during the summer season and spend six weeks or two months in sanatoria among the mountains or by the seashore . . . For a short time the tired, isolated worker can enjoy the society of his own kind; his wife can meet and chat with other housewives; and his children can enjoy the rare pleasure of playing with other children, white like themselves. These resorts are cool, the air is pure and invigorating, and the missionary returns from them in September feeling fresh and strong, ready to take up with renewed vigor his arduous labors.[1]

In the days before the Meiji Restoration, Karuizawa, built on a high plateau, had been a flourishing town straddling the Nakasendo, one of the great roads running between Kyoto and Tokyo and along which endless processions of daimyo, or feudal lords, used to journey. Since the daimyo had lost power and ceased to travel the Nakasendo, the people of the town had fallen on hard times and were therefore grateful for the missionaries' patronage.

It is not difficult to understand why the foreigners liked Karuizawa. Sitting on the verandas of their wooden houses, they could enjoy lovely views through endless green pines up to the mountains, which were dominated by a smoking volcano, Mount Asama. In 1906 it was estimated that over a thousand foreigners took their holiday in Karuizawa. They stayed in pleasant wooden shanties which were dotted all over the plain, which, the American writer Arthur Lloyd noted in *Every Day Japan*, gave the place the appearance of a newly established ranching centre on the foot-hill prairies of Saskatchewan or Alberta.

The missionaries were well organised. A housing committee allocated accommodation, managed golf links and stables, and organized tennis tournaments, picnics, and walking parties. In 1904 the public-welfare committee was able to report that "several objectionable rubbish heaps had been removed, roads repaired, and the police had promised to take steps for providing more jinrikishas during the summer." Certain foreigners had been requested to take better care of their dogs, which had been causing annoyance to fellow residents. That same year the *Japan Weekly Mail* reported that the tennis tournament was followed by a ping-pong tournament hosted by Hannah, whose "lavish hospitality and unwearying attention to her guests day after day will be long remembered by

Karuizawa pleasure-seekers." Such generous entertaining, not to mention the chair with four coolies that was in attendance each day, gave people the strong impression that Hannah Riddell was a lady of substantial private means.

Tradesmen from Tokyo found it well worth their while to spend July and August in Karuizawa, attending to the summer tourists' needs. Many of the lady missionaries lived in remote places and were especially delighted with the dressmaker's shop, where they could buy new bonnets and replenish their wardrobes. Hannah used to turn out her own cupboard each summer before going to Karuizawa and give the hospital patients the clothes she no longer needed, returning to Kumamoto in September with some smart new outfits.

But as the missionaries would have been the first to point out, their time at Karuizawa was not all spent in pursuing pure pleasure. The summer months were also used for conferences, quiet days, and intellectual gatherings. Karuizawa was an oasis for lonely missionaries, and those two months in the fresh cool mountain air, apart from reviving them physically, probably saved many of their number from mental and spiritual breakdown.

CHAPTER 25

New Horizons

Although Hannah's efforts had received official praise and recognition she knew that the hospital's existence remained precarious and that the day when she would be able to relax her publicity campaign or fund-raising activities was a long way off. By 1907 she was considering how best to lobby support from a wider public and at the same time expand her work beyond Kumamoto. She rightly focussed on the United States as a likely and lucrative source of income. On 15 March she wrote to Count Okuma yet again seeking his help:

> I am planning to leave Kobe for the United States on 3 April. While I am there, I am thinking of explaining to a small number of people about the importance of relief of lepers and about the Kaishun Hospital, using the drawing-rooms of kind, understanding peoples' homes.
>
> I am also thinking of making an appeal to the general public with a request for donations.
>
> I am so sorry for troubling you but would you be good enough to drop a line, to introduce me to influential American people you know and to your other friends and acquaintances there? I should also be grateful if two or three friends of yours here could introduce me to their friends in the United States.
>
> Being a complete stranger there, I should like to avoid giving

people there any unnecessary anxiety or misunderstanding about me. I am so sorry for troubling you but I should be most grateful for anything you can do for me on the above matters.

Hannah knew many missionaries from the United States both through Ada, who had already been working with the Americans for seven years, and through contact with them at Karuizawa. But she shrewdly judged that introductions made by Count Okuma and his high-powered friends would open doors to the drawing-rooms of much wealthier citizens than those offered by her missionary friends.

The strategy Hannah outlined in her letter to Okuma proved so effective that by 1910 contributions from America and Canada amounted to forty-four percent of all donations and were coming from almost every state in the Union. Although Hannah's personal relationships often went disastrously wrong, she had an extraordinary flair for public relations and over the years built up an astonishingly impressive network of support for the hospital.

The contributors listed in the accounts read like an international *Who's Who*— Augusta Countess Ferrers, Count C. H. Bentinck, Princess Oyama, Mrs. Barrett Browning, Mrs. Fulton Cutting, Lady Lindsey Darling, Archbishop Sweatman (Primate of Canada), Sir Ernest Satow, Mrs. Oliver Peabody, William Keswick MP, Sir John Buchanan Riddell Bart, Princess Iwakura—to name but a few. The most illustrious of all her patrons was Empress Teimei, the wife of Emperor Taisho, who in 1916 gave the then magnificent sum of six thousand yen to the hospital and who continued to regularly and generously support Hannah's work (and all those involved in the fight against leprosy) after she became the Empress Dowager. The 1925 accounts show that the Japanese Home Office also supported Hannah and in that year gave the handsome sum of 4,598 yen.

In 1910, although donations were pouring in from across the Atlantic and from England, back in Japan they had all but dried up, amounting that year to a meagre six percent of all contributions. Hannah was forced to take her begging bowl yet again to Shibusawa but it was once too often even for the generous Viscount. Not unreasonably Shibusawa told Hannah that he was actively trying to raise money for his own hospital and could not ask his friends to give money simultaneously to two institutions. Furthermore, he argued that now that five state leprosaria were being built there was little further need for the Kaishun Hospital to continue.

The normally composed Hannah responded with tears to this hard-line reasoning, protesting that her patients were of an entirely different calibre from the tramps and vagrants found in the state hospitals and could not be expected to live with them. Although sympathetic, Shibusawa stood firm, believing that social welfare was the responsibility of government and should not rely on the goodwill of individuals. For Hannah, it was a bitter moment. She had thrown herself wholeheartedly into the cause of the Japanese leper, fully expecting it to be her life's work. Now she was being told by her most effective supporter, albeit very kindly, that her role was redundant.

To make matters worse, support for the Kaishun Hospital among the foreign community was also waning but for a very different reason, as the *Japan Weekly Mail* made plain in an article published on 12 March 1910:

> Another visitor well known to Tokyo is Miss Riddell who is now staying at the Hotel Metropole. Miss Riddell is well known in Japan, England, and America for her persistent advocacy of the cause of the Japanese leper, and it is but recently that she returned from a prolonged tour in England and America, where she had been working up sympathy for her noble institution at Kumamoto. The foreign communities in the larger cities of Japan have never been backward in helping along any good cause and there is, I know, much interest felt among us for the unfortunate class for whose benefit Miss Riddell has devoted her life. But the foreign merchant in Japan is nowadays very far from being a merchant-prince, and for the rest the time is coming into measurable distance when we shall have to pay an extra 30 sen on every pound of imported butter, a corresponding increase on every tin of condensed milk, and a general rise in prices which will make living almost a forbidden luxury to foreigners with restricted incomes. It is to be hoped that the hardness of living will not dry up the springs of Christian charity, but it may do so, and the philanthropist will have to make provision for this danger to his supplies.

Hannah certainly did her best to make provision and was never short of ideas for raising money. There was the calendar with its pretty illustra-

43. Empress Dowager Teimei, who gave generously to the Kaishun Hospital over many years, photographed in 1931.

44. *Left:* Female patients taking exercise together in the grounds of the hospital. In the wheelchair is Aiko Tamaki, who was born into a wealthy Osaka family and contracted leprosy from her maid.

46. *Facing page, above:* Eight patients who were baptised by the Bishop of London on the day of his visit.

45. The laboratory at the Kaishun Hospital. Looking through the microscope is Matsuke Miyazaki, at that time a student at the Fifth Higher School. He later became director of the Keifu-en state leprosarium.

47. Hannah with the Bishop of London and other members of his party in December 1926. Hannah had used an imperial donation to put up a sun-dial in commemoration of the Crown Prince's wedding in 1924.

48. *Left:* Hannah shortly before she died in 1932. In the background is the church which she herself designed.

49. *Below:* Hannah's funeral on 6 February 1932. The coffin was carried by some of the younger patients.

50. *Facing page, above:* Ada and the hospital staff in the early 1930s.

51. *Facing page, below:* Ada with a Special Messenger from Empress Dowager Teimei and his entourage.

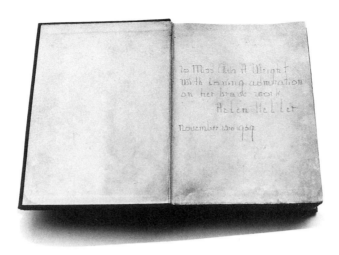

52. *Facing page, above:* A dedication from Helen Keller written in 1937.

53. *Facing page, below:* The closure of the Kaishun Hospital on 3 February 1941, nine years to the day after Hannah's death.

54. *Right:* Ada in 1948 with the children of leprosy patients.

55. *Below:* Ada shortly before her death in 1950.

56. The author talking to former patients of the Kaishun Hospital.

57. The ceremony held in Kumamoto in April 1993 to mark the inauguration of the Riddell-Wright Memorial Society.

tion of the hospital's Christmas decorations, a New Year's stamp, and the Daily Bread League. To become a member of the Daily Bread League, the donor was invited to commemorate some personal anniversary by contributing a whole day's supply of food for the patients. The ladies of the American and British Embassies gave charity balls, and concerts were held at the Imperial Hotel. The amateur entertainment put on for the hospital's endowment fund by the Tokyo Musical and Dramatic Association was given full coverage by the *Japan Weekly Mail*, which reported as follows:

> Indeed it was a notable event. Mr. Brady had no fewer than five turns, for being imperatively recalled after "Tink-a-Tin" he gave "Blue Ribbon Jane" which if possible eclipsed his other songs and fairly brought down the house. "A Pair of Lunatics" went splendidly and the Tableaux Vivants and Dance by Young Ladies of Tora-no-mon School were excellently performed.

Despite all Hannah's valiant and imaginative efforts, it seemed that external events quite outside her control were always conspiring to defeat her purpose. In 1914 the Great War broke out, and English and American concern for Japanese lepers quickly evaporated. Hannah, ill with worry and arthritis, came close to a nervous breakdown and took to her bed. A newspaper picked up the story, and it was soon generally assumed that she had contracted leprosy. On hearing this dire news, the assistant station-master at the Kumamoto railway station immediately put up a notice requesting donations from the railway workers. The large sum which he proudly presented to Hannah must have achieved more than any medicine to restore her health and morale.

Further help came from another unexpected quarter. Sanji Muto was president of the largest spinning company in the country, Kanebo, Ltd., based in Osaka, and business was going well. While Europe was engulfed in a terrible war, Japan was experiencing an economic boom. Muto had at times been a modest subscriber to the hospital and on the strength of this Hannah contacted him when she was in Kobe. Moved by her tale, Muto immediately went into action. He spoke publicly in support of Hannah's work, organised large meetings, and personally lobbied his friends, many of whom had recently become rich from shipping and other war-related industries, pressing them to contribute to the hospital. He was so successful that in a comparatively short time he raised a sum of money equal to all the overseas donations Hannah had received before the war.

Despite the labours of such noble individuals, it was a precarious existence for the hospital and at no point in her career was Hannah able to let up on her fund-raising efforts. At the advanced age of seventy-two, she made her final trip to the United States, a journey which, combined with a visit to England, lasted more than a year and must have cost her considerable physical effort. The whimsical letter she wrote on 3 May 1928 from the Murray Hill Hotel, New York, to her beloved dogs, suggests she was anxious to get home to Japan:

> My dear Lady Pixie Lord Bobs and Patricia
>
> Today I saw a picture which I hope may interest you and Aunt Ada as much as it has interested me.
>
> Thank you very much for all the loving messages you have sent me; I hope that before very long we may have the joy of meeting face to face, and you <u>cannot imagine</u> how much I am looking forward to that.
>
> Please give Bonnie much love and many kindly rubs with your dear noses, and tell Tobias that I quite look forward to making his honourable acquaintance.
>
> Please give my yoroshiku [best wishes] to all the servants who have been so kind to you. I do hope we shall all have a lovely time in Karuizawa and that you will all try not to bark too much!
>
> From your loving and longing "Missis" and "step-missis"
>
> PS A little Pom used to pass my room twice a day when I was unable to move in Philadelphia and I tried to hear it bark. Tell Auntie Ada that I had so much love and humanity shown one. Heaps of flowers every day and food and cushions and all manner of nice things. HR

The reference to "all the servants" in this letter is no surprise. An old Japanese lady, still very much alive in 1994, lived as a child in the house opposite Hannah's. She vividly remembers there being not only a large number of servants at 436 Furushinyashiki but also a cook and a butler. By 1928 the jinrikisha that had carried Hannah daily to and from the hospital (from which she was once toppled out when some boys poked a stick in the wheels) had been replaced by a black chauffeur-driven car. At that date cars were still a rarity in Kumamoto. When it arrived at the door to collect Hannah, she always emerged from the house accompanied by two of her black Pomeranians—perhaps Lord Bobs and Lady Pixie.

Hannah was clearly sensitive to the fact that she was regarded with some misgiving by her immediate neighbours. When during her absence one of her dogs had to be restrained by the maid for barking viciously at the sister of a prominent neighbour, Hannah was quick to react. She donned a black *haori* (a formal short jacket worn over kimono) and went round to his house to apologise in person.

Any local suspicion directed at Hannah was, at least in part, caused by her sheer extravagance. Indeed, given the hospital's roller-coaster financial existence, it is hardly surprising that Hannah's fine lifestyle raised some eyebrows. It was generally assumed that she had private money but in fact her income came from hospital funds. Exactly how large a salary she gave herself is difficult to say, since the surviving annual accounts are organised into very broad expense categories such as "sundries" and "travel" and "expenses for foreign staff." In fairness, it should be noted that the accounts were always checked by professional auditors. And if the silks, servants, and chauffeurs did not fit in with everyone's view of how a lady missionary should conduct her affairs, Hannah herself seems to have been quite untroubled by any questions of probity concerning her personal expenditures. She was convinced that living the life of a grand lady was the only way she would be accepted as an equal by those who had the means to keep the hospital going. In this assertion she was almost certainly right, and it did at least give her the moral justification to follow her natural inclinations.

It was probably Count Okuma who first planted the idea in Hannah's mind that she should carry the fight against leprosy to other parts of Japan. As early as 1901 she had visited Kusatsu, a mountain village not far from Karuizawa and about a thousand miles from Kumamoto. Straggling down a narrow ravine, it was a picturesque village of beautifully carved wooden houses reminiscent of Swiss chalets.

Like Kumamoto, Kusatsu had become a mecca for lepers but in this northern village it was not a temple but hot springs which drew them. *Murray's Handbook to Japan* reported that the springs were "especially efficacious—not only in rheumatism, and, as discovered by Dr. Baelz, in gout—but in syphilis, leprosy, and other loathsome diseases." The lower part of the town was reserved entirely for lepers but, *Terry's Japanese*

Empire noted, "the visitor need have no fear of contagion (possibly only after long and frequent intercourse), as the sulphurous and (other chemical and diabolical) stenches that hiss out from the seething subterraneous furnace below it act as correctives and curatives. Few places of the world will remind one so much of what one imagines the nether world to be like."

CHAPTER 26

Waters of Hell

The waters, pouring out of fissures in the volcanic rock, were directed through bamboo pipes to primitive bathhouses. In some place the rocks were stained with copper streaks, vitriolic blues, brilliant yellows, and jade greens, which were quite dazzling in bright sunshine, but this beauty was deceptive. Inside the baths human beings voluntarily underwent the kind of torture normally depicted only in artistic visions of a fiery hell. At the bath used by the lepers, it was reported that "the sights and the human misery one witnesses there are so repulsive, and are such a drain on one's sentiment, that squeamish persons had better stay away."[1] The average temperature of the water was about 125 degrees Fahrenheit and, as the following graphic description makes clear, immersion was a very unpleasant experience:

> When all is ready a bath attendant goes out into the street and blows several long blasts on a brass horn and soon the bathers are seen ambling painfully across the square. In the bathhouse they mount to a platform which rises round the central pools and disrobe to a thin white shirt or tunic. From forty to sixty can enter the pools at one time, and when this batch is out a second group is admitted. All bathers must submit to a sort of semi-military discipline, and must enter and leave the water together, at the word of command of the bath master. The ratio of men and women is about four to one.

Against the walls, in racks like cue-racks in a billiard-room, stand scores of deal boards about 8 ft long and 1 ft wide; each man takes one of these, all range themselves in a row around the outer edges of the sunken pools. A curious performance now begins and lasts for twenty to twenty-five minutes. One end of the plank is dipped into the water and by a deft wrist-motion a corner is lifted and with it about a gallon or more of water, which is flopped to one side with a splash; then the other side is raised with a like result, the rim of the pool giving forth; meanwhile a resounding smack as the plank strikes it, first on one edge, then on the other. In a minute or two a concerted rhythm is attained, bodies begin to sway in unison, and to the forty or more resounding whacks is added a vocal chant which soon rises to a roar. The sound of the voices and the noise made by the water and the boards is deafening. Air is supposed to enter the holes made in the water and to cool it—bringing the temperature down from about 135 F to 125 F. The spirit of joyousness evoked by the rhythmical shouting and by the belief that they are beating the heat out of their common enemy inspires the bathers (now in a lather of perspiration) with a sort of Dutch courage, which, be it said, does not evaporate when they slip their tender bodies into the scalding liquid . . . At another signal the bathers—who are now joined by women who have taken no part in the cooling opera-tion—kneel in rows along the beams and pour each a hundred or more big dippers full of the hot water over their heads and necks—to prevent congestion and syncope on entering the water. By this time rising steam has filled the room with a thick gray mist, and any clothing seems as heavy as if one were in a Turkish bath. Many of the naked backs of the bathers show moxa scars as big as a silver 50c [cent] piece usually near the spine . . .

Suddenly the stentorian voice of the bath master asks if all are ready. The last vestige of clothing is now whipped off hastily, twisted into a bundle and thrown to the platform, and primitive Japan is represented by youth and manhood, matrons and maidenhood, fat and slender, winsome and otherwise, who lower themselves slowly into the almost boiling water, until lines of shiny black polls and slowly purpling faces only are to be seen above the boards. A silence like that of the grave ensues, and is broken only by the loud ticking of the time-clock and the echo of splashing boards and chants and roars in other near-by baths. The bath master now tells them they will have to stand the ordeal but three short minutes, and he chants a sort of deliberate doggerel, to animate them. An anguished *ai* of lamentation or a rippling moan is the only response these three minutes mean, almost an eternity to the exquisitely tender, sore-flecked bodies into which the hot acid is biting zestfully, but the Japanese suffer it with accustomed fortitude. When, at the end of the first minute, which in the tense silence seems much longer, the bath master assures them that but two minutes remain, a thin cheer surcharged with eager agony ripples through the room. The clock ticks with awful slowness, and when the prompter tells them there remains but a single minute a score of parboiled bodies almost pop out of the water, so vehement is the response. Not a few of the grim faces look as if they could not stand the ordeal a split second longer, much less a minute. But they do, and with the final ringing shout, "Get out of the water s-l-o-w-l-y," starting at a point high up in the scale and descending to a rich basso profundo, the threescore bodies rise like corks that have been held below the surface, and with such amazing unity that it would be a good watch that could register the fraction of time between the first and the last.[2]

The writer of this passage was anxious to allay any fears his English and American readers may have harboured on the subject of mixed bathing:

The stranger unfamiliar with the time-honoured customs of rural Japan will be impressed curiously by the promiscuous bathing of the sexes in all the baths, but he cannot fail to note the natural decorum which everywhere prevails. He may also wish to remember the statement of a witty writer, to the effect that "in Japan the nude is seen but not looked at." If this be borne in mind, one will have no difficulty in gaining admission as a spectator; cameras and note-books are, however, excluded.[3]

It is unlikely that Hannah ever went inside these baths as she deeply disapproved of mixed bathing but she did make several journeys to Kusatsu, where she found large numbers of lepers living in "vice and idleness depending on their friends," she wrote afterwards in a religous pamphlet. Twelve years would pass before she finally had enough money

{ 175 }

to send a Japanese priest out from Kumamoto to start missionary work among the Kusatsu lepers, but he was so successful that Hannah was able to report, with obvious delight, that not only had nine of the ten saké shops closed but the obscene songs habitually sung by the lepers in the hot springs had been replaced with hymns. Her proudest boast was the victory over "that most deeply rooted evil among the lepers of Kusatsu viz: gambling." One of the two men masterminding the gambling operations in town had become a Christian and the other had been forced to open a shop for pickles when his previous clientele had evaporated under the influence of Christianity.

It is not Hannah, however, who is chiefly remembered for good works among the Kusatsu lepers but another Englishwoman and one of a very different temperament and character—Mary Cornwall-Legh. Described by Lois Johnson Erickson in *Highways and Byways in Japan* as "tall, sweet and gentle, with brown eyes which have seen such suffering that the shadow of it lingers in them," Mary was everything that Hannah was not. Hannah had been forced to struggle hard for all that she had achieved in her life but Mary was born into an aristocratic family, had a degree from St. Andrew's University, and a substantial private income. It was not until 1908, when she was already fifty-one, that Mary felt free enough from her responsibilities in England to travel to Japan, where she took up work as an independent missionary loosely attached to The Society for the Propagation of the Gospel. In 1914 she began her work with the lepers of Kusatsu in the St. Barnabas Mission. Two years later the mission was allocated to the American diocese and Mary Cornwall-Legh formally appointed by Bishop McKim to take charge of it.

She bought some land and built herself a house where she lived throughout the year despite the bitterly cold winters and total isolation from her fellow Westerners. During the winter months she refused to heat her house with anything more than a charcoal fire-box, confessing that if her own home were warm, she would not be able to bring herself to enter the lepers' houses or the freezing cold church. The lepers wandered freely in and out of her house and the fact that she happily shared meals with them astonished some American ladies who visited her in 1925. Mary told them that she considered it vital to mingle with the people in order to succeed and that she would have happily become a leper herself if it would have helped her work.[4]

Indeed, Mary Cornwall-Legh's whole approach to the care of lepers was in marked contrast to Hannah's. Over the years, largely using her own resources, she gradually built several schools, a hospital, and a small library. One of the American ladies described the scene as it was in 1925:

> The leper carpenter buys his supplies from a leper green-grocer; the grocer gets his clothing from a dry-goods merchant, also a leper, and so, through the community . . . Everywhere there are lepers—beside our car, sitting in the wide-open houses, helping to put up new buildings, pushing carts, running sewing-machines, going about their business or loafing gloriously. Heads bald, eyebrows gone, faces swollen, smitten with blindness and disfigured with thick black eruptions, they look much alike. Here and there we see some whose hands or feet are gone, whose noses are nothing but a gaping hole.[5]

There were separate homes for men and women and, significantly, houses for couples and families as well. Mary's strategy of encouraging the lepers to marry and to live as normal a life as possible was in direct contradiction to Hannah's strict segregationist policy as well as her view that lepers should live in a calm, protected environment doing as little work as possible. Under the circumstances, it was as well that Kusatsu and Kumamoto were a thousand miles apart.

Hannah had been working with lepers for over twenty years when Mary took charge of the St. Barnabas Mission and she did not welcome any challenges to her authority on the subject. One man who knew both ladies extremely well, the Reverend Alfred Hewlett, wrote of Hannah that "she seems to lose no opportunity of running down, to put it mildly, and indeed hindering, I regret to say, the work here, which is 1000 miles off from Kumamoto whether of Miss Cornwall-Legh's or my own."[6]

Alfred Hewlett, like Mary Cornwall-Legh, was a late-comer to missionary work, having spent most of his life as a parish priest in England. Inspired by the example of Father Damien, who had impressed the world with his work among the lepers in Hawaii and who eventually succumbed to leprosy himself, Hewlett had decided at the late age of fifty-eight to devote the rest of his life to working with the lepers of Japan. In 1914, at the very moment Europe was plunged into the Great War, Hewlett had headed out east on the Trans-Siberian Railway, enduring a thoroughly uncomfortable and often dangerous journey for several weeks with little to eat.

On arriving in Japan, Hewlett went straight to Kumamoto and spent the following three years working at the Kaishun Hospital. He was remembered there with great affection by the patients in the magazine *The Mission Field* as "our sympathetic friend and Pastor [and] while with us we felt that we had in him a father." He may have been close to the lepers but his relationship with Hannah was fraught, and the underlying reasons causing the tension between them are not difficult to discern. Since Hannah had resigned from the CMS fifteen years earlier, she had been accustomed to having complete charge of the hospital and being its undisputed figurehead. Hewlett, a man and an ordained priest, had come to Kumamoto with the sole purpose of working with lepers and no doubt soon formed ideas of his own about how best to do this, ideas that did not necessarily acquiesce with Hannah's. Matters finally came to an acrimonious head over the administration of the leper fund. Hewlett was a purist and in his view too much money was spent on items not directly concerned with the patients' welfare. It was not the first time such criticism had been directed at Hannah and she did not like it.

In 1917 Hewlett left the Kaishun Hospital amid much bitterness and moved to Tokyo but he spent a large part of each year in Kusatsu working with Mary Cornwall-Legh. There he found, according to one SPG report, "plenty of work to be done and noble and devoted Miss M. H. Cornwall-Legh, who has been doing a most efficient and successful work . . . the lepers love her and trust her implicitly." But it seems that in this case absence succeeded in making hearts grow fonder. In 1923 Hewlett wrote to the SPG back in England that while he was in Kusatsu with Miss Cornwall-Legh, they had "had a very pleasant visit from Miss Riddell" and he hoped that all past differences were now "forgiven and forgotten."

27

Okinawa

By 1923, when Hewlett was describing Hannah's last visit to Kusatsu, she had already tried and failed to send effective help to the lepers living in Okinawa, a place where they were harshly treated by the local population. Most of them lived as true outcasts in crude beach huts, surviving as best they could on seaweed and sweet potatoes.

But in 1927 Hannah found just the man for the task of serving the lepers in Okinawa. Keisai Aoki, a leper and a devout Christian, had spent a number of years in a state leprosarium before being admitted to the Kaishun Hospital. Initially he had been very happy in his new surroundings but his contentment had been shattered when he fell in love. The object of his passion, Aiko Tamaki, was thirty-two but looked ten years younger. She had difficulty with her feet and hands and could not even manage her own hair but she did have some education and a particularly sweet nature. Well aware of the strict rules of the hospital and Hannah's rigorous views on love affairs between the patients, Keisai never dared to declare his feelings to Aiko, although he continued to love her all his life.

He had to conceal his pleasure when one of the women patients fell sick and he was provided with an excuse to visit their ward and see his beloved Aiko. "Miss Riddell cared for us as one would a tropical flower in a greenhouse . . . but the hospital had become not only a greenhouse to me but also a place of torture. I was so near the one I longed for so much but could not approach," he wrote in *Mission to Okinawa*. The last straw for Keisai was the appearance in the hospital of a rival. When Hannah asked him to go to Okinawa and undertake missionary work there with the lepers, he thankfully accepted. All the patients, Aiko among them, gathered to see him off from the Kaishun one cloudy February day. His last glimpse of her was leaning on the shoulder of a leper friend, waving him goodbye, her eyes full of tears.

Keisai carried with him Hannah's parting words: "Don't visit women patients and don't get married . . . working as a missionary is your life. If you continue on in faith, keeping yourself pure and remaining single all your life, the glory of God will be upon you more and more."[1] It was a tough command and one that, much later in life, Keisai regretted having followed so diligently.

If Aoki was looking for distraction from his broken heart he certainly found it in Okinawa, where he lived and preached among the lepers in appalling conditions. But the misery he encountered was punctuated with lighter moments, especially the fishing expeditions on which he accompanied his new friends. The waters around Okinawa are beautifully clear and teeming with exotic fish. Lepers who found it hard to walk on land moved with grace and ease underwater, where they could stay for several minutes until finally emerging with octopus, eel, or cuttlefish pinned to their harpoons.

The lepers were also highly skilled in managing canoes which they dug out from cedar or pine trees, as Aoki wrote in *Mission to Okinawa*:

> As the sail filled in the strong wind, one of them pulled on the tight rope tied to his disabled hand. And when it seemed that canvas might split under the strain, he leaned far over the gunwale, his body almost touching the water as he hung grimly on. It was so daring and thrilling that it chilled us to watch. Another had a paddle tied to his hand with cords and with this he steered our course so effectively that it was like an acrobat show.

There was a disaster one day when Keisai and his friends were over-turned in the surf. They survived unharmed but lost their precious boat. On hearing of the catastrophe, Hannah immediately sent enough money to buy a new one, a spontaneous act of generosity that was entirely typical of her. Hannah was keenly interested in Keisai's progress and he in turn reported to her regularly. Her letters would be brought to him in his hovel by an elderly woman who, in order to reach him, had to struggle along a ridge path, through farms and stony fields, and finally down a precipitous cliff.

> My dear child,
> I was glad to receive your letter and delighted to know that you are strong, keeping well, and have started your work. Your body is not only your own. It is a precious body set aside to serve the Lord by doing His prepared work. Be careful not to catch a cold. Avoid chills while sleeping. I pray for you and all the leper friends in Okinawa every day.
> I am sending your salary for April by money order. Please accept it . . .

To succeed in his mission, Keisai came rapidly to the conclusion that he needed two things—money to buy some land where the lepers could live and farm for themselves and a bicycle. To his surprise and disappointment Hannah refused both requests. She argued that the procedures for buying land were too complex to be practical and that the lepers would not be able to farm and cope with the frequent typhoons without making their health much worse. And the bicycle was simply much too dangerous for him. Hannah told Keisai that he was engaged on a vital mission and if he were to have an accident there would be no one to carry on his work. Although at the time Keisai was deeply annoyed by her refusal, he later interpreted it as an example of her deep affection and her motherly concern for him.

Keisai's reaction was generous because on both counts Hannah's reasoning was questionable. The lepers of Okinawa could hardly have lived a more miserable existence than they did already, and by establishing their own community they would at least have given themselves a chance of a better life. Furthermore, the whole project would have cost ridiculously little, as land in Okinawa was extremely cheap. To refuse Keisai a bicycle because of the risk to his well-being was also absurd, as his health was constantly being damaged by the huge distances he had been forced to cover on foot.

Why did Hannah react in such a perverse manner? Her genuine commitment and devotion to the lepers are never in doubt but, as she had proved so often before with both her actions and words, she wanted to manage things in her own way and, above all, she wanted to be in control. If Keisai's scheme had succeeded, the Okinawa leper community would inevitably have developed along different lines to the Kaishun Hospital and Hannah's influence on it would have quickly faded.

At least the saga of the bicycle had a happy ending. Bravely ignoring Hannah's negative reaction, Keisai bought a cheap secondhand bicycle with his own resources and painfully taught himself how to ride it on the beach, picking up many cuts and bruises in the process. He eventually plucked up the courage to confess his revolutionary behaviour to Hannah and was surprised by her response. Not only did she raise no objection but from that time onwards was always quick to send him money when his precious transport needed repairing. Then came the ultimate endorsement. A ladies' bicycle (still a great rarity in Okinawa) and painted a vivid red suddenly appeared outside Keisai's hut—a present from Hannah. For nearly five years they regularly corresponded with each other until 3 February 1932, when Keisai received a telegram:

Mother passed into heaven at 1:10 P.M.—KAISHUN

Hannah was dead.

28

Old Age

Although the financial problems of the hospital were never far distant, the last ten years of Hannah's life were lit by the comfortable glow of success and recognition. She had become a celebrity who commanded respect and admiration not only in Japan but also in England and America. Furthermore, in 1923, her beloved Ada finally gave up working for the Americans and settled permanently at 436 Furushinyashiki, where she soon absorbed much of the daily burden of running the hospital and household.

Hannah, herself the daughter of a soldier of the British Empire, was every inch an imperialist, and her deepening links with the Japanese Imperial Family in her later years gave her particular pleasure. In the alcove of her drawing-room hung portraits of the Emperor and Empress at the time of their coronation, complimented by portraits of King George V and Queen Mary hanging over her desk. When Emperor Meiji died in 1912 Hannah had written an emotional letter to the Empress Dowager:

> Madam
>   Having lived in this beautiful land for twenty-two years, may I be permitted to endeavour to express my deep and heartfelt sympathy with your Imperial Majesty on this especial day of trial—the final parting, the last sad journey.
>   The hearts of all Englishwomen will be sympathising with your

Majesty today. Indisposition prevents my being in Tokyo to express in person my sorrow and sympathy, but the evening hours will be spent in fervent prayer that your Most Gracious and Beloved Imperial Majesty and all the Imperial Family may be embued [*sic.*] with fortitude in this hour of grievous trial, and experience both hope and consolation in the loneliness of sorrow.

Your Majesty's most humble servant,

H. Riddell

Imperial support for Hannah's work was made very public in 1922, when she was awarded the Sixth Class Order of the Sacred Treasure. This second award (the first was the Medal of the Blue Ribbon) underscored just how much her efforts had come to be appreciated by the Japanese. For Hannah this honour symbolised the great distance she had travelled—physically, of course—but also socially and spiritually from her modest beginnings in the barracks at Barnet.

In 1924 Hannah received some money from the Imperial Family to mark the occasion of the Crown Prince's wedding. Instead of putting it into the hospital's general fund, she used it to erect a sun-dial, a reference to the Crown Prince as the heir to the Empire of the Rising Sun, exactly the sort of imaginative gesture that was typical of her. The sun-dial was the object of great interest among the Japanese, and one visitor wrote the following:

Of all that I saw, the thing that I liked best was the sun-dial. It may be foolish to say I admired the sun-dial when I had gone to see the Hospital but where is there another hospital so restful and pleasing in Japan? At a time when most hospitals were thinking only of how they should cut down expenses, this one has erected a sun-dial which reminded me of those I saw in England, which are in front of churches or at the entrance to country houses.

I called that place a corner of England, which pleased Miss Riddell very much . . . I only wished that the church had been built of stone and was covered with ivy; then I could have sat on one of the steps and read Gray's "Elegy" . . . I hope that poets will choose "Sun-dial" as the name for the collection of poems dedicated to Miss Riddell.[1]

Visitors flocked to the Kaishun Hospital in Hannah's twilight years and she clearly basked in their interest and admiration. One of the more distinguished foreigners to make the pilgrimage to Kumamoto was the Bishop of London. The latter had taken over from the Bishop of Liverpool as president of the hospital in 1916 and ten years later arrived in Japan. He very nearly missed Kumamoto altogether but persuaded the captain of his steamer to make an unscheduled stop at Moji, enabling him to spend a few hours at the Kaishun before rejoining his ship.

There was a fever of activity in the hospital preceding the great occasion of the bishop's visit. When one of the patients made a speech in English to welcome him, Hannah stood by "beaming with a mother's pleasure at the cleverness of her child."[2] After the bishop had toured the hospital and baptised a number of the patients, he was escorted out into the bitter cold of the December night by the lepers, all of them carrying Japanese lanterns. The choir sang hymns until his car finally vanished into the darkness.[3] The bishop's visit was an emotional event and, for Hannah, the ultimate vindication of her role in the bitter battles thirty years earlier with Bishop Evington and the other English missionaries.

Despite the diabetes which dogged Hannah during her final years she continued to entertain the many visitors who called on her at 436 Furushinyashiki with her usual elegance. One of these, the Director of the Gotemba Leper Hospital, Father Iwashita, visited her in 1929, when she was seventy-three, and later wrote a graphic account of the occasion. Although it was mid April and the cherry blossom was in full bloom, a fire was burning in the drawing-room, which he recalled as being furnished in a clever blend of Japanese and Western styles. He nervously sipped the tea brought to him by a maid until, warned of Hannah's imminent appearance by the rustlings of her dress, he leapt to his feet to meet her. Still immense in stature and dressed in her customary black from head to foot, she greeted him in the manner of "a queen receiving a loyal subject."[4]

Hannah at once set about informing him of all the things she considered wrong with the Gotemba hospital. Intelligently picking up his cue, Iwashita explained that the only reason he had come to see her was to seek her advice. Once this important point had been established, she smiled for the first time and immediately invited him to lunch. Iwashita was deeply impressed by her knowledge and experience, and their conversation went splendidly until he foolishly quoted a view concerning sex segregation that differed from her own, thus opening once more the flood-gates of disapproval. Hannah may have been elderly and infirm but her old passions and prejudices were not in the least diminished.

In 1927 Hannah showed great courage by undertaking a long and arduous fund-raising journey to Europe and America. In an interview she gave to the *Japan Advertiser* just before her departure, it is clear that she realised that this visit to England would be her last:

> I am not as young as I was; time passes fast; whether I shall have another opportunity to visit England I do not know. I have much business to attend to and there are many people I intend to call upon. But then I shall come back here and resume my work.

When she did return the following year, her health was already in serious decline. By the spring of 1930 she was suffering from neuralgia and from so much pain in her knees that she was forced to move around in a wheelchair. A long stay in Karuizawa improved her health and the following November she managed to visit the Empress Dowager in her palace in Tokyo. On 13 December she wrote to her old friend and ally Viscount Shibusawa from the Imperial Hotel:

> Dear Viscount Shibusawa,
>
> Although I have been at this Hotel since November 8th, I have been quite unable to pay my respects to you because I have been ill all the time having two Doctors and two nurses. Now, however, I hope to be able to travel about 18th, and am very anxious to reach Kumamoto by Christmas.
>
> There were several things I greatly hoped to have had an opportunity of talking to you about, but it is now I fear, impossible.
>
> Please take great care of yourself as the cold weather comes on.
>
> With kindest regards, and many thanks for all your courtesy when I was last in Tokyo.
>
> Believe me,
> Ever Sincerely Yours
> H. Riddell[5]

Despite Shibusawa's great age—he was ninety years old—Hannah had been clearly anxious to talk business with him. She was also forced to refuse an invitation to attend a dinner given by the Minister of Home Affairs and must have been seriously ill to turn down such a valuable opportunity to press her cause among so many men of influence.

There was a temporary improvement in her health but by the summer of 1931 she was ill again. That November, however, on the occasion of some important military manoeuvres Emperor Showa spent a few days in Kumamoto. Hannah was informed that the Imperial Chamberlain, Isaburo Yamagata, would visit the hospital, provided all the patients remained out of sight in their rooms. Hannah sent back the spirited reply that under such conditions she could not possibly accept the chamberlain's call. Once again she had made her point and at the same time achieved her goal: Yamagata did go to the hospital but the patients were not confined to their rooms.

Hannah was too ill to attend the imperial banquet but on 13 November the Emperor received her in the prefectural office. To prepare for the audience, she spent several hours practising deep bows in the Japanese style but when actually standing in front of him, her bowing technique deserted her and instead she found herself, despite her neuralgia, dropping a curtsey. It was fitting that this great event should have been her last major public engagement.

At ten past one on the afternoon of 3 February 1932 Hannah died. On hearing the news of her death, the stunned patients gathered in the family room of the hospital, where they tried to absorb the fact that "Mother" had left them. Their leader quoted John 14:18: "I will not leave you desolate; I will come unto you." Weeping filled the room. Two days later all the patients were there to see the hearse pass slowly by the Fifth Higher School and to watch Hannah enter the gates of the hospital for the last time. The coffin was placed in front of the family room, and one by one they went up to it to bid her goodbye. According to a patient who recorded the events in his diary, "it was a most pitiful sight to see the blind led to the coffin."[6]

The funeral, which took place the next day, was a touching affair and would have greatly pleased Hannah. At three o'clock, to the tolling of the church bell, her coffin was carried to the church by the younger lepers, who were followed by the other patients, all of them carrying flowers. The church was overflowing with flowers and wreaths (made by the patients) and after the service, conducted by the Bishop of Kyushu, Arthur Lea, some two hundred telegrams and letters of condolence were read out. The coffin was borne to the crematorium and was followed by a long procession of mourners, many of them lepers who were not usually permitted to go beyond the gates, one of whom wrote the following description:

> Despite the mist on the banks of the River Shirakawa, the setting sun shone on the water. In the west, Mount Kimpo was clearly visible and far away to the east Mount Aso stood as if in silent prayer. At the crematorium the service ended with prayers in English and we looked for the last time on all that was mortal of Miss Hannah Riddell. Loneliness, solitude, and silence covered the Hospital that night.[7]

CHAPTER 29

Hard Times

In 1923 a simple stone mausoleum had been built in the gardens of the hospital. Its presence brought great comfort to the patients, who until that time rarely knew what would happen to their remains. Because they were lepers, their families often refused to accept their ashes, a fact that added yet further grief to their stricken lives.

Hannah had no doubts about where she wanted her own ashes to lie. In 1918 she had told a senior government official, "I am working as a Japanese and shall continue to do so until I die. I desire my ashes to remain on Japanese soil."[1] Six months before she died, Hannah visited the crematorium to make sure it had the facilities to cope with someone as large as herself. Her wishes were respected and her ashes duly transferred into a metal box, painted with her name under a small cross, and placed on a shelf in the mausoleum alongside those of many of the Kaishun patients.

The obituaries, published in numerous Japanese papers as well as the London *Times*, the Baltimore *Sun*, and many others, were generous in their praise. Hannah would have been delighted, not just because she would have enjoyed all the flattering things written about her achievements but also because of the excellent publicity the hospital received as a result.

It is sad that Hannah died before the cure for leprosy was discovered, but in some respects it was as well that her death occurred when it did.

Times were changing dramatically and for foreigners life in Japan during the 1930s had become increasingly difficult, as Ada was soon to find out.

It was on her slender shoulders that responsibility for the Kaishun Hospital now fell, and Ada Wright was a very different human being from her aunt. Although fifteen years younger than Hannah, many Japanese thought Ada was actually older, perhaps because her hair had already turned grey by the time she was fifty. She was slight, seemingly frail, and, unlike her aunt who always kept strict outward control of her emotions, she readily gave way to her feelings. Hannah, never a consensus operator, expected her wishes and commands to be executed without discussion, but the patients knew that they could always negotiate with the more approachable Ada. One of them wrote a haiku summing up the differences between the two women. In the poem, big decisive Hannah was compared to a rose and Ada, small and quiet, to a violet.

Ada hero-worshipped her aunt and was much too modest to think she could ever attempt to take her place. (She jokingly referred to herself as the lepers' "stepmother.") But she was nevertheless determined not to squander Hannah's legacy and to continue the work of the hospital along the lines that had been so clearly set out. She soon settled into a daily routine of morning worship in the church, then did chores, wrote letters, and kept the accounts. Lunch was at 11 A.M., supper at 4 P.M., and each evening she toured the patients' rooms to chat with everyone and ensure that all was well.

Ada may have been a more pliable personality than Hannah but she continued to enforce the strict segregation rules when she became director of the hospital. Only one patient, a young boy, was allowed free access to both the male and female wards and as a result was often entrusted to carry fan letters from the men to a famous lady poet, Haruko Tsuda, who was for some years resident in the hospital.

The patients may not have liked segregation but they were pleased when in 1933 it was decided they should be paid a small sum of money for any work they undertook. Aiko Tamaki, the young woman with whom Keisai Aoki had fallen in love, subsequently published an article expressing her delight at being rewarded for her efforts. A teacher, touched by what she read, offered to send the ladies at the hospital money to buy something they needed and the ladies decided upon a sewing-machine. This simple transaction caused a major stir in the hospital's usually calm atmosphere. To everyone's astonishment, when Ada heard about the sewing-machine she responded angrily, apparently furious that the patients should have acted so independently.

Such behaviour from the normally gentle Ada was strangely out of character and a clear indication of just how much the strain of running the hospital was beginning to tell on her. As the 1930s progressed and Japan's relations with the West grew steadily worse, donations for the hospital dwindled to a trickle of their former flow. Basic supplies of food and medicine became harder to acquire and inevitably standards dropped.

Ada was lucky, at least, to have a staunch ally in Jingo Tobimatsu. Tobimatsu had worked as chief administrator at the hospital since 1915 and, having faithfully served Hannah for seventeen years, he now gave his total support to Ada. It is hard to imagine how she would have survived in the aftermath of her aunt's death without him. In 1934 he published a memoir of Hannah in which he made clear his devotion to her and the hospital, a loyalty that was to cost him his life.

Ada's anxieties over the hospital were heightened by her increasing loneliness. All her life Hannah had been the centre of her world and now that "Auntie" was gone there was an emotional void that no one else could fill. Furthermore, Hannah had always dictated policy and made all decisions, leaving Ada in the role of willing executor. But suddenly, and just at the age when most of her contemporaries' thoughts were turning to retirement, Ada found the fate of the hospital entirely in her hands. She did, however, possess a strong streak of stubbornness which combined with her unquestionable courage helped her survive the years ahead.

During these difficult times, Ada was befriended by Masao Sawa, a young Japanese teacher of English. His grandmother had known Ada in Mito when she was working with the American missionaries and Sawa's friendship proved a lifeline. Every Sunday Ada used to invite him to lunch after church, delighted at the end of a long lonely week to have someone with whom she could speak English. He came to know her very well—her love of reading (everything from A. A. Milne to Virginia Woolf), her love of English flowers (including the daffodils she had planted in the hospital's front garden), and her strong dislike of American accents.

But it was soon apparent to Sawa that his social calls on Ada were being carefully monitored by the authorities. As the political climate changed and police surveillance was stepped up, people who regularly used to visit Ada stopped, leaving only Sawa, the Reverend Namio

Toyofuku, from the Anglican church, Dr. Reiju Fukuda (who had attended Hannah in her last illness), and a handful of other faithful friends to sustain her morale.

This increasing isolation, together with the stark economic realities of her life, eventually convinced Ada to give up the house at Furushin-yashiki—her home base for more than thirty years—to live in the hospital. By 1934 the laboratory was no longer functioning and in that year a floor was added to the original building to provide Ada with living quarters. Police harassment did not cease, however, after her move to the hospital and by 1940, after the outbreak of the Second World War in Europe, she was being watched round the clock. Strangely enough, the authorities made no objection when she went to Karuizawa that summer for what proved to be her last visit there.

But when Ada returned on 11 September she had an unpleasant shock. Not only were there detectives in her house but Tobimatsu had been imprisoned. The police were suspicious because he had taken the trouble, partly under Hannah's influence, to educate his five daughters to an unusually high standard. Nor could the police understand how he could afford to do so on his salary as the superintendent of such a lowly institution as a leper hospital. Even more damning were the numerous English books they found in his house. Ada spent many hours at the police-station trying to secure his release and even offered to take his place in jail. He was detained for three months and returned home a shadow of his former self. He never fully recovered from his ordeal and died before the end of the war.

During that autumn all Ada's incoming letters were opened and she had to ask permission to send any out. She was permitted to receive visitors only in the presence of a police-officer and then forced to converse in Japanese. The police, anxious to expose her espionage activities, searched her rooms for evidence. They soon discovered her wireless and at once accused her of using it to receive secret messages. It was the same radio on which she had listened to the funeral service of George V in 1936, an event that had moved her to tears. When the Japanese authorities confiscated this precious possession, they severed her last remaining link with the outside world. The days of The Policeman and Warders' Friend were a distant and ironic memory.

Even the calendars sold at Christmas were deemed a violation of the Publication Act. Ada was further accused of making money out of the wicked propaganda she circulated abroad, with which, the police charged, she was claiming that Japan was populated by people scarred with the most shameful and loathsome disease in existence. The screw was tightened yet further when the account books of the hospital were seized and Ada was unable to draw money out of the bank. Finally, on 13 January 1941 the board of trustees met to discuss the situation and came to the only possible decision they could—the hospital had to close.

By coincidence, the final day of the Kaishun's existence was also the ninth anniversary of Hannah's death, 3 February 1941. At ten o'clock, *manjū*, sweet buns that were a rare treat in wartime Japan, were delivered to the hospital as Ada's farewell present to all the patients. But before they had a chance to eat them, the patients were summoned to assemble in front of the chapel, where Dr. Fukuda, a Christian doctor and a longtime supporter of Hannah and Ada, gave a talk on the history of the hospital lasting almost an hour.

When he had finished, Dr. Matsuke Miyazaki, director of the local state leprosarium and also a loyal friend of Ada, announced that in a few minutes, at 11:30 A.M., the Kaishun Hospital would close and the patients would be removed to his hospital, the Keifu-en. At these words Ada broke down in tears. The patients were sent to collect their belongings but as they returned to their rooms they saw men in white coats already carrying out any moveable objects. The police had been mobilised to watch them and ensure that no one escaped. Just before 11:30 the patients boarded the open trucks. After forty-six years of existence, the Kaishun Hospital was no more.

At the very moment the convoy moved off, Ada stumbled and, hanging on to the back of one of the trucks, was dragged forward, crying, "I am sorry, I am so sorry." When the vehicle stopped briefly at the gate, her fingers had to be prised off it one by one. As the lepers waved goodbye to the diminutive figure standing so folornly at the entrance, they began to sing a hymn, "God is the Refuge of his Saints." The *manjū* remained uneaten.

CHAPTER 30

Pain and Healing

By March 1941 the Consul-general in Nagasaki and Ada were the only two English people still living in Kyushu. Ada had little choice but to obey the British Embassy's evacuation order and on 24 March, her last day in Kumamoto, she made a final tour of the deserted hospital. Dr. Miyazaki had come to see her off, and he recorded her parting words as she was getting into the car. She said she was old and had no idea where she would die. But whatever happened to her, she would make sure that her ashes were sent to him and she asked him to promise that he would place them in the mausoleum alongside those of her aunt and the lepers of the Kaishun Hospital.

Ada would have liked to return to England but was deterred by the prospect of crossing a sea infested with enemy submarines. She decided therefore to go to Australia, where May Freeth had offered to share with her a small house she was moving to near Perth. She and May had known each other since their early twenties when they had both been students at The Willows, and both women had lived in Japan for more than forty years.

May Freeth's missionary endeavours had been largely concentrated in the region around Mount Aso, where she had funded the building of a church and started a number of nursery schools. She too had been forced to leave her life's work, and in the harrowing days of late 1940 had stayed for a time at the Kaishun Hospital. Six of May's Japanese friends gave her a set of kimonos as a parting gift and had gathered at the hospital to present them to her, as one of the women later recalled:

> We dedicated our farewell prayer together in tears. I helped her dress in the kimono, from undergarments to the foot covers on her geta. She was so pleased that she went around all the wards showing off her kimono. It took me a long time to help her dress because her build was different from that of a Japanese woman. I can still feel the warmth of her body in my hands. As I dressed her I could not hold back my tears, knowing we would probably never meet again.[1]

It was some solace to Ada to know that she would be spending her remaining days with an old friend and one with whom she had so much shared experience, but nothing could compensate for the misery of being forced to leave Japan in such tragic circumstances. At the age of seventy-one and with almost no money, Ada had to face up to starting again in a completely new country.

On 1 April, already aboard the *Tokyo maru* waiting to sail from Kobe, she received an unexpected telegram from the Empress Dowager, who wrote, "I truly offer my deepest sympathy for having to close the Hospital that you have run for so many years. I thank you for your great contribution to leper relief work in Japan." After receipt of this imperial telegram, Ada was treated with great courtesy by the crew despite being an enemy alien. Ada treasured the telegram until the end of her life. It was a welcome ray of comfort in an otherwise gloomy world.

Guildford, the small town ten miles to the northeast of Perth where Ada lived for the next seven years, was in every way different from Kumamoto. A few years before she arrived, one Guildford citizen had stood in court accused of keeping the town awake all night by allowing his four hundred cattle to roam down the main street and graze by the railway station. In his defence he retorted, "I did not think anything could wake Guildford up. It has been asleep since I knew it."[2] May's brother taught at the grammar school and for his retirement had built a pleasant house, which he generously made available to his sister and her friend. One Freeth relative noted that they arranged it like a Japanese house with hardly any furniture and despite their age always slept on the floor.

Ada left little account of her years in Perth. She spent much of her time involved with her church, St. Matthew's, with the Women's Auxiliary in Perth, and in correspondence with friends in England, America, and Canada, as the meticulous record she kept of letters she sent and received makes clear. After the war, when she was able to resume contact with her Japanese friends, her first letter was to Dr. Miyazaki to find out how each of the former fifty-nine Kaishun patients had survived the war. Ada had not for one moment given up hope of returning to Japan and repeatedly applied to the Australian authorities for the necessary papers but was always turned down.

In December 1946 May died and Ada was left quite alone. Apart from her sorrow at losing her companion, Ada found herself in an awkward position. The house belonged to May's brother and although there was no question of his turning her out, now that his sister had died, he not unreasonably wanted it back.

Ada resolutely continued to write to the town hall in Perth until one day, answering a knock at the door, she found the mayor himself standing on her doorstep, curious to meet this obsessed old lady who besieged him with requests to go to Japan. He pointed out that firstly she was seventy-eight and secondly, that if she went to Japan so soon after the war, she might well be attacked. Ada assured him that it was unthinkable anyone would hurt her, but that even were she to be killed the moment she stepped on Japanese soil, she would at least die happy. The mayor had met Ada's stubborn streak. He sensibly capitulated and signed the needed document on the spot.

Guildford gave her a fine send-off. In St. Matthew's "Abide with Me" was sung especially for her at evensong, which was followed by a party in the parish hall with cakes, tea, speeches, and gifts. Sometime in the early summer of 1948, Ada disembarked at Kobe, the same port at which Hannah had arrived nearly sixty years before. Her appearance made newspaper headlines and Masao Sawa, living then in Oita and himself only recently returned to Japan from a Russian labour camp, quickly contacted her in the hotel. She told him of her plans to go to Kyushu as soon as possible, and on 11 June she arrived at Kumamoto by train. Dr. Miyazaki was on the platform to meet her, and before long Ada was standing on the very spot where she had made her dramatic farewell to the patients seven years earlier. Except for the laboratory building, the hospital had disappeared without trace but in its place the Tatsudaryo, a home for the uninfected children of leprosy patients, had been built by the Tofu Foundation, the leprosy-prevention organisation to which Ada had donated the hospital's assets when she left Japan. On 27 June she wrote a joyful letter to the Empress Dowager:

> Your Imperial Majesty
>
> It is with a heart full of gratitude that I send this line to inform your Majesty that I am once again back in Kumamoto after being away in Australia for a little over seven years. I am home here now to stay, and pray that the months or years God gives me, may be used even in a little way, in comforting and helping our sadly affected brothers and sisters. All the years I have had to be away from Japan, your Majesty and the Imperial Family were ever in my thoughts and prayers.
>
> I have greatly treasured the very kind telegram your Majesty graciously had sent me when I was leaving Kobe in 1941.
>
> Praying that God will abundantly reward and bless your Majesty for many kndnesses
>
> I am,
Your humble servant
Ada Hannah Wright

Although Ada's house was still standing, inside it had been completely wrecked, with even the curtain rods having been torn out. Dr. Miyazaki decided she should live in what had once been the doctor's house, and it was there that Ada spent her final months. Of the many kind gestures made to her when she arrived back, one of the most touching was the return of some of the furniture she had been forced to sell before her departure. Indeed her friends were anxious to make things as easy and comfortable for her as possible but in postwar Japan life was difficult for everyone and there were few available resources. Ada's financial problems were finally eased when Dr. Miyazaki persuaded the Tofu Foundation to give her a monthly allowance.

At last Ada was back where she belonged and the diary that she kept during her last months suggests that she found contentment. One of her chief pleasures was her daily contact with the forty or so children of the leprosy patients with whom she often played and to whom she always gave the sweets she received from abroad. She regularly took the bus to the Keifu-en, where she spent happy hours with her friends, the former

Kaishun patients. She attended church there every Sunday, even in the heat of the summer when she shielded herself from the fierce sun with her broken umbrella, one of the few possessions she still owned that had belonged to Hannah. The days of maids were long since past and although her friends kept an affectionate eye on her she was able to manage most things for herself.

Ada was always an enthusiastic recorder of birthdays and anniversaries and on 18 June 1949 she wrote a last letter to her loyal supporter, the Empress Dowager:

> Your Imperial Majesty
>
> It being just over a year since I returned to this my home city of Kumamoto, I want to congratulate your most gracious Majesty on the occasion of your birthday. I pray it may be a very happy day and that your Majesty may yet have many many more years full of blessing and happiness.
>
> This year is also a great occasion for thanksgiving, it being the 40th year since the Government and people decided to work together for the relief of leprosy.
>
> My late Aunt Hannah Riddell who worked so hard that this should come about must be rejoicing in the Heavenly Home, that so much is now being done for the relief of this terrible suffering.
>
> It will indeed be a great day of rejoicing when leprosy is quite stamped out.
>
> May God our Heavenly Father bless every effort being made for the alleviation of this disease.
>
> Again wishing your gracious Majesty every joy and many, many happy years to come
>
> I am,
>
> Your humble servant
>
> Ada Hannah Wright

The final entry in her diary, made on Monday, 31 October 1949, is a typical one:

> Fine but very cold. Dr. Hayashi of the Sensho-en called having taken a patient to the Tairo-en [a Catholic leprosarium in Kumamoto founded in 1898 which survived the war and in 1995 still had

{ 198 }

fourteen patients]. In the early afternoon did some post office money business and bought some white chrysanthemums for the *nōkotsudō* [family vault], tomorrow being All Saints Day. Rheumatism quite bad in my right leg, not easy to walk.

At the beginning of 1950 Ada became very weak and was confined to bed. She politely refused treatment from a doctor attached to the allied forces, saying that she was being very well cared for by the Japanese. Realising that she was near to death, she requested that she might be allowed to give a farewell message to the lepers of Japan. NHK, the national public broadcasting organization, granted her wish and on 21 February 1950, Ada's frail voice crackled over the wireless:

> Dear Friends, how are you getting along these days? I hope you are doing well. I remember all of you in my prayers every day.
> I stayed in Australia during the war but my heart was always with you in Japan. I should like to see you, but I am sorry I am too weak to leave my bed. I hope and pray that you will continue to have faith in our Lord's cross and resurrection. Please be good children of God. I am looking forward to seeing you again in heaven.

Shortly after her eightieth birthday, on 26 February 1950, Ada died. According to her wishes, her ashes were placed in the Kaishun Hospital mausoleum, close to those of many of the lepers and next to those of her aunt. The two caskets containing their ashes are identical, except that Hannah's is twice as big as Ada's.

* * *

Hannah was a big person—big in every sense of the word—and would have made her presence felt wherever she had chosen to live. God or fate or chance took her to Japan and the fact that she is remembered there with such admiration and affection, when most of her English missionary contemporaries have been long since forgotten, speaks for itself.

Hannah was no scientist. She did not find a cure for leprosy, nor would her theories on segregation receive any support today. What she did do, despite all the obstacles she faced, both logistic and man-made, was to focus attention on a terrible human tragedy. With the force of her personality she made people sit up and take notice. And by her personal example and sheer determination she compelled them to think more compassionately and constructively about the victims of leprosy. What is more, she achieved all this despite being both a foreigner and a woman.

One day on a whim, I sent a sample of Hannah's handwriting via a friend to a graphologist, Amanda Clarkson. I have never met the lady nor have we ever spoken or discussed Hannah. It would, however, be hard to improve on her analysis of Hannah's character based on the scrap of paper I sent her:

> The writer is <u>conservative</u> and has respect for tradition. She is duty-bound, practical, logical, rational, down-to-earth, organised, and well-adjusted. She has warmth and amiability but this may be controlled. She also has sociability and a strong personality—one to be reckoned with. She has underlying determination and persever-ance—and a sense of humour.

Hannah would be pleased.

Postscript

In 1957 the children's home where Ada had spent so much time in her final months was closed and with it disappeared one of the last real links with the Kaishun Hospital. But it was not the end of the story. On the site where the hospital had once stood a home for the aged was built and in 1970 was renamed the Riddell-Wright Memorial Home. A few years later, in 1976, Dr. Mamoru Uchida published a collection of reminiscences contributed by various people who had known Hannah and Ada and worked closely with them. And there was more to come.

In April 1993, nine months after my husband and I arrived in Japan, I travelled with the wife of the then Foreign Secretary, Judy Hurd, to Kumamoto, where she had been invited to inaugurate the Riddell-Wright Memorial Society. At the time neither of us had ever heard of the two ladies, and as we flew past the snow-capped peak of Mount Fuji we had to concentrate on our briefs.

We were driven from Kumamoto Airport in a fleet of cars furnished with red carpets and lacy anti-macassars to the auditorium where the ceremony was to take place. The Japanese know how to arrange such occasions with sincerity and style. There was a brightly uniformed brass band, a large school choir, television cameras, newspaper photographers, and a hall packed with an enthusiastic audience. Up on the platform were seated, on one side, distinguished citizens of Kumamoto, and on the other, the British contingent. Above us, dominating the proceedings, hung two huge photographs of Hannah and Ada.

It was a happy day. We enjoyed the receptions, the speeches, the cherry blossom, and especially the chance to look around the museum which had been newly set up in Ada's old quarters above the laboratory, the only building in the Kaishun complex to survive. There, carefully displayed, were some of Hannah's and Ada's clothes and books (including a volume inscribed by Helen Keller given when she visited the hospital in 1937), various documents, a much-labelled trunk, an organ, and a Union Jack lovingly sewn together from odd pieces of material. That evening, during the splendid dinner jointly hosted by the brand new Riddell-Wright Memorial Society and the equally new Japan-British Society of Kumamoto, Professor Masao Sawa, Ada's close friend, moved many of those present to tears with an emotional address on the subject of the ladies and their work.

But when I returned to Tokyo the next day, I forgot all about the English missionaries as I became caught up once more in the endless whirl of embassy life. A couple of weeks later I received a letter from the Kumamoto historian Keishi Fujimoto, asking me if I could help the Riddell-Wright Memorial Society find out more about Hannah and Ada. There were some large gaps in their information, and almost nothing was known of the ladies' lives before they arrived in Japan. I put the letter in my pending tray.

Before long, I received a reproachful note from a Japanese friend in the embassy, also interested in the history of Hannah and Ada. He pointed out that as the wife of an ambassador I was, by definition, an ephemeral creature and would be quickly forgotten. I had, however, been given the chance to do something useful by researching this intriguing story and it was high time that I got on with it.

How glad I am that I did. In the process of trying to unravel Hannah's and Ada's lives I learned a great deal—about Japan certainly, but also about England and especially about the two countries' early contacts with each other. I even learned something new about my own family. Edward Cropper, the first president of the Kaishun Hospital, and his daughter, Evelyn, who lived and worked with Hannah in Kumamoto for several years, are my forbears, and my Cropper cousins are today our close neighbours in the north of England.

Not long after we arrived in Japan, Morihiro Hosokawa, whose family had done so much to support the Kaishun Hospital, was much in the news and in September 1993 he became Prime Minister. His election caused a

sensation, breaking as it did, the LDP's forty-year monopoly on government. It was an exciting moment in Japanese politics and the novelty of
the situation was reflected at a banquet hosted by the Hosokawas for John
and Norma Major, the British Prime Minister and his wife, when many of
the guests present expressed surprise at the relaxed and informal atmosphere. That evening, hearing of my interest in Kumamoto, Mrs. Hosokawa invited me to stay with her on my next visit there, an invitation I was
glad to accept.

The entrance to the Hosokawa estate is shaded by an avenue of
majestic cedars. I entered the compound through a traditional Japanese
gate flanked by a long low wall and found myself before the Shinto shrine
which, in deference to the Emperor, had replaced the earlier Buddhist
temple after the Meiji Restoration. Some distance from the shrine stood
the house itself, originally built as a pavilion where members of the family
could rest when visiting their ancestors' tombs.

On that warm October day, the *shōji* screens were drawn back, leaving
the front of the house open to the garden and revealing a classic Japanese
interior. A long lacquer table had been set for lunch, and Mrs. Hosokawa
had gathered together for my benefit all those interested in the history of
Hannah and Ada and their hospital. We knelt on cushions at the table
and while we ate looked out across the garden to the shrine and trees
beyond and to where the Kaishun Hospital had once stood.

On another visit to Kumamoto, I asked my city-government hosts if I
might see No. 2 Choanji-cho, where Hannah, Grace, and later Ada spent
their first few years in Japan. We set off in a large posse equipped with
nineteenth-century town plans. We soon found the street, almost under
the shadow of the reconstructed castle. At one end of Choanji-cho is a
pretty shrine and at the other a McDonald's, and between them a mixture
of old houses and fashionable boutiques. The street is narrow and, despite
the uninspiring car park that runs along one side, still retains some
charm. It was not so hard to imagine the three ladies living there
although, sadly, no trace of their house survives. There was an uncomfortable moment when we realised that, unusually in Japan, none of us was
carrying a camera. However, all was well when we spotted a vending
machine selling disposable cameras right next to where Hannah once
lived. As Hannah herself was an enthusiastic photographer, she might
even have approved of this typical manifestation of the late twentieth
century.

Around the corner from Choanji-cho is one of the places where she and her fellow missionaries used to regularly preach. The area is now enclosed by a glossy shopping arcade and on the spot where Hannah liked to stand was a group of busking musicians covered in tattoos and jangling metal.

Sadly, there is also nothing left of the fine house in Furushinyashiki where Hannah lived for over thirty years. The house was destroyed in the war, and its site is currently occupied by a playground, the river embankment has been built up with concrete, and the wooden bridges replaced by ugly metal structures.

The old Fifth Higher School, next-door to the site of Kaishun Hospital, has survived in tact, although now forms just a part of the greatly expanded Kumamoto University. Built of red brick and stone, it is a particularly handsome example of Meiji architecture and rightly designated an Important Cultural Property. The building houses the university museum and displays the fiendishly difficult English examination papers prepared by Lafcadio Hearn and Natsume Soseki. It is hardly surprising that their students needed to go to Hannah's house in Choanji-cho for extra tuition.

Even the then Mayor of Kumamoto, Yasumoto Tajiri, found the time to help me. We walked together along the narrow lanes that run behind what used to be the Kaishun Hospital and the Fifth Higher School and where Ada had invariably walked each day. He remembered regularly meeting her on his way to school as she was returning to the hospital from the bakery. In 1940 he was a small boy and unaware of the complexities of war. He did not see in Ada a potential enemy, only a kind old lady to whom he always bowed respectfully as she passed by.

Once when I visited Kumamoto, I was taken late at night to the top of Hanaokayama, the hill which Captain Jane's fervent young Christians ascended to make their solemn vow. It was the same hill that John Brandram also used to climb and from where he anxiously viewed his vast territory so depressingly full of unconverted souls. Today a wide tarmac road leads to the summit, where there stands a Buddhist stupa and where on warm summer nights young couples also look out across the city lights unaware of the dramas enacted here, absorbed with different concerns.

In my efforts to trace the story of Hannah and Ada, my most touching encounter was with the former patients of the Kaishun Hospital. We gathered together one day in the Keifu-en, where they have lived for over fifty years and where today there are still nearly nine hundred inhabitants. Their disease has long since been cured but after years of institutional living they prefer to remain in the hospital, which has extensive grounds, shops, and even *karaoke*. Despite their considerable age, Kenji Amano, Eizo Maeda, Tomiko Kawabata, and Shizuko Nakamura remembered the events of all those years ago as if they happened yesterday. They vividly described to me their memories of the hospital, of Ada, and of that dramatic day in 1941 when the Kaishun venture finally came to an end.

To say that much has changed in Japan since Hannah's day is to state the obvious. But there are some things that endure, especially the Japanese ability to forge deep and lasting friendships. Such friendships even span the generations, as I discovered when the descendents of Hannah's and Ada's friends in turn became my friends. The Ogasawara family is a perfect example of such continuity. The Reverend Saburo Ogasawara was one of Ada's most loyal supporters in the difficult days before the war, and his son-in-law, Yoshiaki, a small-business owner, left property that was later sold, the proceeds of which were used for the reconstruction of the Riddell-Wright Memorial Home on the site where the Kaishun Hospital once stood. Today his son, Dr. Yoshisuke Ogasawara, who, together with Yukio Furuki, director of the home, conceived the idea of a memorial society for Hannah and Ada, works unpaid several days a week at the home. I visited Kumamoto often and my experiences there with the people and places I came to know so well are among my happiest memories of Japan.

If today, a hundred years after the Kaishun Hospital first opened its doors, there is much in Kumamoto that Hannah would not recognise, there is at least one place that she knew well which is little changed—the Honmyoji temple. These days, however, its magnificent flight of steps flanked by hundreds of ancient stone lanterns is no longer defaced by the human misery which affected Hannah so deeply. The very peace and tranquillity which now surrounds the temple is in itself a monument to her achievement.

Notes

Chapter 1
[1] Natsume, Soseki. *Nikki Oyobi Dampen*. Vol. 13, *Soseki Zenshu*. Tokyo: Iwanami Shoten, 1985.

Chapter 2
[1] Bereton, J. M. *The British Soldier: a Social History from 1661 to the Present Day*. London: Bodley Head, 1986.
[2] The Registry for Births and Deaths, St. Catherine's House, London.
[3] Roberts, Lord Frederick. *Forty-one Years in India: from Subaltern to Commander-in-Chief*. London: Bentley and Son, 1897.
[4] Muster lists of the 26th Regiment of Foot, the Cameronians. Public Record Office, Kew.

Chapter 4
[1] Simey, Margaret. *Charity Rediscovered*. Liverpool: Liverpool University Press, 1951.
[2] Armstrong, Richard Acland. *The Deadly Shame of Liverpool*. N.p., 1890.
[3] *The Liverpool Review*. 31 March 1888.
[4] S. C. Potter, "The Social Origins and Recruitment of English Protestant Missionaries in the Nineteenth Century." (Ph. D. diss., London University, 1974).

Chapter 5
[1] *Church Missionary Society Intelligencer*. "Japanese Notes." Feb. 1891.
[2] Archives of the CMS, Birmingham University, Birmingham, England.
[3] Gordon, M. L. *An American Missionary in Japan*. Boston: Houghton Mifflin, 1892.
[4] *Church Missionary Society Intelligencer*. Aug. 1890.
[5] Tristram, H. B. *Rambles in Japan*. London: The Religious Tract Society, 1895.

Chapter 6
[1] Moule, G. H. *The Spirit of Japan*. London: Church Missionary Society, 1913.
[2] Ibid.
[3] Ibid.
[4] Ibid.

Chapter 7
[1] Gordon, M. L. *An American Missionary in Japan*. Boston: Houghton Mifflin, 1892.
[2] Ibid.
[3] Bird, Isabella. *Unbeaten Tracks in Japan*. London: John Murray, 1880.
[4] Stock, Eugene. *History of the CMS*. London: Church Missionary Society, 1899.

Chapter 8
[1] Sladen, Douglas. *The Japs at Home*. London: Hutchinson and Company, 1892. Anderson, Isabel. *The Spell of Japan*. Boston: The Colonial Press, C. H. Simonds, 1914.
[2] *Terry's Japanese Empire*. Boston: Houghton Mifflin Company, 1919.
[3] Page, Jesse. *Japan: Its People and Missions*. London: S. W. Partridge and Company, 1895.
[4] Ibid.
[5] Arnold, Alfreda. *Church Work in Japan*. London: The Society for the Propagation of the Gospel, 1905.

Chapter 9
[1] Hearn, Lafcadio. *Out of the East*. Boston: Houghton Mifflin, 1897.
[2] Ibid.
[3] Bickersteth, Mary. *Japan as We Saw It*. London: Sampson Low Marston, 1893.
[4] Gordon, M. L. *An American Missionary in Japan*. Boston: Houghton Mifflin, 1892.
[5] Ibid.
[6] Ibid.
[7] Arnold, Alfreda. *Church Work in Japan*. London: The Society for the Propagation of the Gospel, 1905.
[8] *Extracts from the Annual Letters*. London: Church Missionary Society, 1902.
[9] Hunter, Janet E. *The Emergence of Modern Japan*. London: Longman, 1989.
[10] Hearn, Lafcadio. *Out of the East*. Boston: Houghton Mifflin Company, 1897.
[11] Ibid.

Chapter 10
[1] Griffis, William Elliot. *The Mikado's Empire*. New York: Harper and Brothers, 1877.
[2] Browne, S. G. *Leprosy in the Bible*. 3rd. ed. London: Christian Medical Fellowship, 1979.
[3] Ibid.
[4] *Leprosy*. N.p.: Hastings and Convit, 1995.
[5] Jopling, W. H., and A. C. McDougall. *Handbook of Leprosy*. Oxford, London, Melbourne, and Auckland: Heinemann Medical Publishing, 1971.

Chapter 11
[1] *Church Missionary Society Intelligencer*. "Japanese Notes." Feb. 1891.
[2] Ibid. Feb. 1890.
[3] Ibid. Aug. 1890.
[4] Ibid. Aug. 1893.

Chapter 12
[1] Bickersteth, Mary. *Japan as We Saw It*. London: Sampson Low Marston, 1893.
[2] Ibid.
[3] Ibid.

[4] Ibid.
[5] Ibid.
[6] Ibid.
[7] Ibid.

Chapter 13
[1] Berry, Katherine Fiske. *A Pioneer Doctor in Old Japan: the Story of John C. Berry, MD*. New York: Fleming H. Revell Company, 1940.

Chapter 15
[1] Archives of the CMS, Birmingham University, Birmingham, England.
[2] *Church Missionary Gleaner*. 2 July 1902.
[3] Archives of the CMS, Birmingham University, Birmingham, England.

Chapter 16
[1] Archives of the CMS, Birmingham University, Birmingham, England.

Chapter 17
[1] Archives of the CMS, Birmingham University, Birmingham, England.
[2] Ibid.
[3] Ibid.

Chapter 19
[1] Stock, Eugene. *History of the CMS*. London: Church Missionary Society, 1899.
[2] *Extracts from the Annual Letters*. London: Church Missionary Society, 1902.

Chapter 20
[1] Stock, Eugene. *History of the CMS*. Vol. 3. London: Church Missionary Society, 1899.
[2] Arnold, Alfreda. *Church Work in Japan*. London: The Society for the Propagation of the Gospel, 1905.
[3] Moule, G. H. *The Spirit of Japan*. London: Church Missionary Society, 1913.
[4] Tobimatsu, Jingo. *Hannah Riddell*. Kumamoto: Eda Hanna Raito, 1934.
[5] Little, Frances. *The Lady of the Decoration*. NewYork: The Century Company, 1908.

Chapter 21
[1] Obata, Kyugoro. *An Interpretation of the Life of Viscount Shibusawa*. Tokyo: Zaidan Hojin Shibusawa Sei-en O Kinen Kai, 1937.
[2] Ibid.
[3] Ibid.

Chapter 22
[1] Aoki, Keisai. *Mission to Okinawa*. Hong Kong: Christian Book Room, n.d.
[2] Aoyama, Shigeru. "Flowers Along a Mud Wall." *Aisei Journal*, May 1994–January 1995.
[3] Ibid.
[4] Ibid.
[5] Uchida, Mamoru. *Yukari no Minoru o Michite—Rideru to Raito no Shogai*. Kumamoto: Rideru-Raito Kinen Rojin Homu, 1990.

[6] Aoki, Keisai. *Mission to Okinawa*. Hong Kong: Christian Book Room, n.d.

Chapter 23
[1] Uchida, Mamoru. *Yukari no Minoru o Michite—Rideru to Raito no Shogai*. Kumamoto: Rideru-Raito Kinen Rojin Homu, 1990.
[2] Tobimatsu, Jingo. *Hannah Riddell*. Kumamoto: Eda Hanna Raito, 1934.
[3] Ibid.
[4] Aoki, Keisai. *Mission to Okinawa*. Hong Kong: Christian Book Room, n.d.
[5] Aoyama, Shigeru. "Flowers Along a Mud Wall." *Aisei Journal*, May 1994–January 1995.
[6] Uchida, Mamoru. *Yukari no Minoru o Michite—Rideru to Raito no Shogai*. Kumamoto: Rideru-Raito Kinen Rojin Homu, 1990.
[7] Aoyama, Shigeru. "Flowers Along a Mud Wall." *Aisei Journal*, May 1994–January 1995.

Chapter 24
[1] Peery, R. P. *The Gist of Japan*. New York: Oliphant, Andersen, and Ferrier, 1897.

Chapter 26
[1] *Terry's Japanese Empire*. Boston: Houghton Mifflin, 1919.
[2] Ibid.
[3] Ibid.
[4] Erickson, Lois Johnson. *Highways and Byways in Japan*. New York: Fleming H. Revell Company, 1929.
[5] Ibid.
[6] Archives of the CMS, Birmingham University, Birmingham, England.

Chapter 27
[1] Aoki, Keisai. *Mission to Okinawa*. Hong Kong: Christian Book Room, n.d.

Chapter 28
[1] Uchida, Mamoru. *Yukari no Minoru o Michite—Rideru to Raito no Shogai*. Kumamoto: Rideru-Raito Kinen Rojin Homu, 1990.
[2] Tobimatsu, Jingo. *Hannah Riddell*. Kumamoto: Eda Hanna Raito, 1934.
[3] Ibid.
[4] Uchida, Mamoru. *Yukari no Minoru o Michite—Rideru to Raito no Shogai*. Kumamoto: Rideru-Raito Kinen Rojin Homu, 1990.
[5] Letter in the possession of the Shibusawa Museum, Tokyo.
[6] Tobimatsu, Jingo. *Hannah Riddell*. Kumamoto: Eda Hanna Raito, 1934.
[7] Ibid.

Chapter 29
[1] Tobimatsu, Jingo. *Hannah Riddell*. Kumamoto: Eda Hanna Raito, 1934.

Chapter 30
[1] Hama, Soejima. *Osanana Kora o Mimoto ni Nihon Seikokai no Hoiku no Genten to Genjo*. Tokyo: Seikokai Shuppan, 1987.
[2] Bourke M. J. *On the Swan*. Perth: University of Western Australia, 1987.

Bibliography

Anderson, Isabel. *The Spell of Japan*. Boston: The Colonial Press, C. H. Simonds Company, 1914.

Aoki, Keisai. *Mission to Okinawa*. Hong Kong: Christian Book Room, n.d.

Armstrong, Richard Acland. *The Deadly Shame of Liverpool*. N.p., 1890.

Arnold, Alfreda. *Church Work in Japan*. London: The Society for the Propagation of the Gospel, 1905.

Barr, Pat. *The Deer Cry Pavilion*. London: Macmillan and Company, Ltd., 1968.

Bereton, J. M. *The British Soldier: a Social History from 1661 to the Present Day*. London: Bodley Head, 1986.

Berry, Katherine Fiske. *A Pioneer Doctor in Old Japan: the Story of John C. Berry, MD*. New York: Fleming H. Revell Company, 1940.

Bickersteth, Mary. *Japan as We Saw It*. London: Sampson Low Marston and Company, 1893.

Bird, Isabella L. *Unbeaten Tracks in Japan*. London: John Murray, 1880.

Bourke, M. J. *On the Swan*. Perth: University of Western Australia, 1987.

Browne, S. G. *Leprosy in the Bible*. 3rd ed. London: Christian Medical Fellowship, 1979.

Checkland, Olive. *Humanitarianism and the Emperor's Japan, 1877–1977*. London: Macmillan Press, Ltd., 1994.

Cortazzi, Hugh. *Victorians in Japan*. London and Atlantic Highlands, N. J.: The Athlone Press, 1987.

Cortazzi, Hugh, ed. *A Diplomat's Wife in Japan: Mary Crawford Fraser*. New York and Tokyo: John Weatherhill, 1982.

Erickson, Lois Johnson. *Highways and Byways in Japan*. New York: Fleming H. Revell Company, 1929.

Fraser, Mrs. Hugh. *A Diplomatist's Wife in Japan*. 1st ed. London: Hutchinson and Company, 1899.

Gordon, M. L. *An American Missionary in Japan*. Boston: Houghton Mifflin Company, 1892.

Griffis, William Elliot. *The Mikado's Empire*. New York: Harper and Brothers, 1877.

Gulick, Sidney. *Evolution of the Japanese*. New York: Fleming H. Revell, 1903.

Hama, Soejima. *Osanana Kora o Mimoto ni Nihon Seikokai no Hoiku no Genten to Genjo*. Tokyo: Seikokai Shuppan, 1987.

Hearn, Lafcadio. *Glimpses of Unfamiliar Japan*. Boston: Houghton Mifflin Company, 1894.

Hearn, Lafcadio. *Out of the East*. 1st ed. Boston: Houghton Mifflin Company, 1897.

Hunter, Janet E. *The Emergence of Modern Japan*. London and New York: Longman, 1989.

Iddittie, Junesay. *Marquis Okuma*. Tokyo: Hokuseido Press, 1956.

Ion, A. Hamish. *The Cross and the Rising Sun*, Vol. 2, *The British Protestant Movement in Japan, Korea, and Taiwan, 1865–1945*. Waterloo, Ont.: Wilfried Laurier University Press, 1993.

Jopling, W. H., and A. C. McDougall. *Handbook of Leprosy*. Oxford, London, Melbourne, and Auckland: Heinemann Medical Publishing, 1971.

Kuno, Akiko. *Unexpected Destinations*. Tokyo: Kodansha International, 1993.

Little, Frances. *The Lady of the Decoration*. New York: The Century Company, 1908.

Moule, G. H. *The Spirit of Japan*. London: Church Missionary Society, 1913.

Murray, John. *Murray's Handbook Japan*. London: John Murray, 1907.

Natsume, Soseki. *Nikki Oyobi Dampen*. Vol. 13, *Soseki Zenshu*. Tokyo: Iwanami Shoten, 1985.

Nikiforuk, Andrew. *The Fourth Horseman: a Short History of Epidemics, Plagues, and other Scourges*. London: Fourth Estate, 1992.

Nish, Ian, ed. *Britain and Japan, Biographical Portraits*. Folkestone, Eng.: Japan Library, 1994.

Obata, Kyugoro. *An Interpretation of the Life of Viscount Shibusawa*. Tokyo: Zaidan Hojin Shibusawa Sei-en O Kinen Kai [Viscount Shibusawa Memorial Foundation, Inc.], 1937.

Page, Jesse. *Japan: Its People and Missions*. London: S. W. Partridge and Company, 1895.

Peery, R. P. *The Gist of Japan*. Edinburgh and London: Oliphant, Anderson, and Ferrier, 1897.

S. C. Potter, "The Social Origins and Recruitment of English Protestant Missionaries in the Nineteenth Century." (Ph.D. diss., London University, 1974).

Roberts, Lord. *Forty-one Years in India: from Subaltern to Commander-in-Chief*. London: Bentley and Son, 1897.

Simey, Margaret. *Charity Rediscovered*. Liverpool: Liverpool University Press, 1992.

Sladen, Douglas. *The Japs at Home*. London: Hutchinson and Company, 1892.

Spiers, E. M. *The Army and Society 1815–1914*. London: Longman, 1980.

Stock, Eugene. *History of the CMS*. London: Church Missionary Society, 1899.

Terry's Japanese Empire. Boston: Houghton Mifflin Company, 1919.

Tobimatsu, Jingo. *Hannah Riddell*. Kumamoto: Eda Hanna Raito, 1937.

Tristram, H. B. *Rambles in Japan*. London: The Religious Tract Society, 1895.

Uchida, Mamoru. *Yukari no Minoru o Michite–Rideru to Raito no Shogai*. Kumamoto: Rideru-Raito Kinen Rojin Homu, 1990.

Wilkes, Paget. *Missionary Joys in Japan*. London: Morgan and Scott LD, 1913.

Acknowledgements

This book would never have been begun—let alone finished—without the help and patience of a great many people.

First and foremost, I want to thank the Honda Motor Company and the Hongkong and Shanghai Banking Corporation for their encouragement, support, and interest in seeing this little-known Anglo-Japanese tale reach a wider public.

In Kumamoto I owe a profound debt to the many people whose enthusiasm and determination to keep alive the memory of Hannah Riddell and Ada Wright are the reasons the book was written:

Mitsuya Nagano, Chairman and President of the Riddell-Wright Memorial Society; Yasuhiko Matsukado, Chairman of the Kumamoto Japan-British Society; Yoshisuke Ogasawara, Deputy Chairman of the Riddell-Wright Memorial Society and Chairman of the Riddell-Wright Old People's Home; Taeko Takami, Deputy Chairman of the Riddell-Wright Memorial Society; the late Masao Sawa, an old friend of Ada Wright's and former university professor; Keishi Fujimoto, Director of the Riddell-Wright Memorial Museum; Ichiro Kikuchi, chief dermatologist at Kikuchi Keifu-en and leprosy historian.

I also want to thank the following people for various forms of assistance:

Yukio Furuki, Hitoshi Hadama, Takashi Hatono, Takaaki Ikai, Songi Ikegami, Kazuko Itakura, Wataru Kashi, Shigeru Kumamaru, Shinji Maruno, Tatsumi Minoshima, Kimiko Miyazaki, Jiro Mizuoka, Yoko Nakayama, Akira Ota, Katsuhiko Sakaguchi, Yasumoto Tajiri, Naoko Takeda, Momoko Williams, Masao Yufu.

I should like to record my special thanks to Seiji Tomishige for taking and donating so many of the photographs in the book. His grandfather, Rihei Tomishige, founded a still flourishing photo studio in Kumamoto, and many of his original prints have been used.

I shall always remember Mrs. Morihiro Hosokawa's warm hospitality and the trouble she took to show me parts of Kumamoto I might never otherwise have discovered.

In England, Christopher Gotto's research and insights were vital to the project. Indeed, without his energetic commitment the project would never have got off the ground. He was entirely responsible for uncovering Hannah Riddell's family history, and without his perseverance Hannah's background would have remained in obscurity.

Much of the material in the book was drawn from The Church Missionary Society archives, now housed in Birmingham University. I was lucky that Rosemary Keen, until recently the society's archivist, agreed to undertake re- search for me. Her knowledge of the workings of the CMS is exhaustive, and she left no stone unturned in pursuit of Hannah and her fellow missionaries.

I am also deeply grateful to The Society for the Propagation of the Gospel for allowing me to use material from its archives at Rhodes House, Oxford, and to Catherine Wakeling and Kenneth Osborne of Partnership House, London, who never failed to respond cheerfully to my endless requests.

Despite a very busy career, Atsuko Kashiwagi undertook the mammoth task of sifting through and translating for me all the relevant Japanese material. Her comments and suggestions were always of the utmost value. Jerry Matsumura gave me unfailing encouragement from the start and was never too busy to help and advise. Lia Beretta's extraordinary knowledge of Meiji Japan, particularly of the contemporary English press, was indispensable. She provided me with dozens of relevant cuttings as well as many insights into the period. Romaine Bamford constantly combed the text for errors, flaws, and defects, and those that remain can be blamed only on me. The historian Michael Cooper, who has lived many years in Japan, made many helpful comments. I owe special thanks to Christo- pher Penn and his family, who provided copies of May Freeth's letters and who encouraged me in so many other ways. Jonathan Folb took time off from his medical studies to answer my questions about leprosy and to undertake research on my behalf in The SPG archives at Rhodes House. Wendy Cope researched Hannah's years in Wales and expertly guided me around Oystermouth, and Patricia Winker gave me great assistance in researching Hannah's months in Liverpool.

I would also like to thank the following people for their help, suggestions, and support:

Tessie Abe, Helen Ballhatchet, John Barker, Michael and Maitou Barrett, Georgina Battiscombe, Phoebe Bentinck, Carmen Blacker, Martin Blaser, Robert Boyd, Stephen Boyd, Peter Boyden, Asa and Susan Briggs, Clare Brown, Brian Burke-Gaffney, Frances Butlin, Amanda Clarkson, Robert Coghlan, James Cropper, Gillian Darley, Sebastian Dobson, Lesley Downer, Thomas Easton, Edwin Green, Jiro Harumi, Reijiro Hattori, Clare Hollingworth, William Honaman, Judy Hurd, Emi Ikebe, Yutaka Kagemori, Yuichi Katoh, Peter Kennerley, Tadateru Konoe, Kyoko Kubota, Akiko Kuno, Hiroaki Matsuzawa, Tetsuro Nakasuga, Timothy Nakayama, Kerry Pocknell, Rod Pryde, Miriam Pyburn, John Riddell, Steve Roder, Shoichi Saba, Antoinette Scopinich, Christian Searle, Cindy Shaw-Stewart, Pauline Simkins, Yukika Sohma, Toyoko Terada, Adrian and Miyoko Thorpe, Andrew Watt, Gordon Williams, Nicholas Willink, William Willink, Hisaaki Yamanouchi, Yo Yuasa.

The Imperial Household Agency, the Japanese Correctional Association, the Nippon Seikokai, the nuns of the Tairo-in, the Shibusawa Memorial Museum, St. Paul's University Library, Tokyo University Library, and Waseda University have given me invaluable assistance.

Lastly, I should like to express my gratitude to the staff of the Charles E. Tuttle Publishing Company for assistance in bringing the project to completion.

PHOTOGRAPH CREDITS

The following individuals and institutions were kind enough to compile and reproduce many of the photographs that appear in the book. Numerals indicate the numbers of the photographs within the signatures:

The British Embassy, Tokyo: 34; Church Missionary Society, London: 8, 14, 16–20, 23; Rikuro Hayashi, Tokyo: 36; Imperial Household Agency, Tokyo: 43; Shibusawa Memorial Museum, Tokyo: 32–33; Tomishige Photo Studio, Kumamoto: 6, 10–11, 13, 15, 21, 28, 30, 37, 44, 46–47; Tsuchiya Photo Studio, Karuizawa: 25; Waseda University (Editorial Department of the University History), Tokyo: 31.